ONE
ON
ONE

The Best Men's
Monologues for the
Nineties

The APPLAUSE ACTING SERIES

ONE ON ONE

The Best Men's Monologues for the Nineties

EDITED BY JACK TEMCHIN

APPLAUSE
NEW YORK • LONDON

From the APPLAUSE ACTING SERIES
An APPLAUSE original.
One on One: The Best Men's Monologues for the Nineties
Copyright © 1993 by Applause Theatre Books

An extension of this copyright notice, together with CAUTION and performance rights information, will be found in the "Play Sources and Acknowledgements" section at the end of the book.

Library of Congress Cataloging-in-Publication Data

One on one: the best men's monologues for the nineties / edited by
    Jack Temchin.
        p.   cm. — (The Applause acting series)
      ISBN 1-55783-151-3 (pbk.) : $7.95
        1. Monologues. 2. Acting. 3. Drama—20th century. I. Temchin,
    Jack. II. Series.
    PN2080.057   1993
    822'.04508—dc20   93-6789
                                                                CIP

Applause Theatre Books
211 West 71 Street, New York, NY 10023
phone: 212-595-4735 fax: 212-721-2856

406 Vale Road, Tonbridge KENT TN9 1XR
phone: 0732 770219 fax: 0732 770219

CONTENTS

"All the World's an Audition"

Everybody in the theater auditions. Even casting directors. The day I spoke to Meg Simon, whose office walls are festooned with the shows she's cast (*Amadeus, M. Butterfly,* and *Conversations with My Father* are a few), she was proudly telling friends that she had won the competition to cast *Angels in America.* The news was particularly sweet since other top casting agents were up for the job. Her entire career up to that moment had been her audition.

At about the same time, Jeff Ash, head of Grey Entertainment Advertising, was nervously waiting to hear if he was going to handle a big show from the West Coast. *He* had auditioned by presenting artwork and a proposed advertising campaign.

Everybody in theater faces his or her own audition. Yes, theater *producers,* too! Stanley Brechner, who runs the American Jewish Theater, before the first preview of every show, utters this prayer: "Please God, don't let it be a total and complete embarrassment." Everybody in the theater is subjected again and again to the rigors of being tested. You're not alone.

Yet there's no denying that you, the actor, face the most terrifying audition of all. It's just you and the listener. It's what your parents meant when they told you life is even harder than that final high school exam. It's a test of your guts and skill.

This introduction will not teach you how to do a job you probably already know how to do: act. Advice on "choosing the monologue," "preparing the monologue," and "presenting the monologue," are just fancy ways of telling you how to act. It's probably a good idea to be suspicious of the kind of acting advice you get from book editors anyway. Let me give you an example.

In 1961, I was fifteen and lucky enough to meet Richard Burton and watch him backstage several times in *Camelot.*

One of the highpoints of that show is a monologue by King Arthur that closes the first act. In it, Arthur realizes that his wife, Guenevere, and his best friend, Lancelot, are in love. But he decides to rise above his anger and act as a king, not a jealous husband. The subtext of this thrilling speech is Arthur's attainment of manhood, something he has been striving for since the beginning of the play.

The first time I saw Burton deliver it from backstage, I was surprised to see the entire cast watching from the wings. I asked someone if this happened a lot. "Every night," he assured me. I knew I was watching the ultimate tribute an actor can receive: the admiration of his peers from the wings.

Now, in the acting-advice business, *preparation* is a sacred prescription. Any teaching guru who would suggest otherwise would be a) labeled a heretic and/or b) out of a job! But every night Burton would disdain the profound preparation rituals we all hear so much about. Instead, Richard Burton prepared for his monologue by sipping a cocktail and talking to friends he invited to come by—people like Lauren Bacall and Jason Robards. Until, on cue, his dresser and friend, Bob Wilson, signaled, "It's time." Burton would calmly take a final sip, put down his drink, put on his cape, nod good-bye to us, walk out of his dressing room, pick up his sword, and step on stage. And deliver! So much for preparation! Afterwards, Burton would immediately return to his dressing room and pick his drink back up, perfectly relaxed. As Burton's own career will attest, martinis may not be the best prescription either. Whatever works for you, I'm not going to prescribe it for you here.

I am going to offer you many monologues to work on.

Both Meg Simon and Randy Carrig, the casting director of the Manhattan Theatre Club, emphasize that the choice of monologue is the single most important clue they have about you as an actor. Simon says it's like introducing yourself at a party. She forms an impression of your tastes and education through the material you choose to perform. While she stresses that she prefers "light audition pieces (suffering by request only)," she really enjoys actors who are part of "new theater...in touch with emerging playwrights." She likes risk-takers.

Carrig goes further about material, saying he often asks who wrote the particular play the monologue is from and what the actor thinks about it. If the actor doesn't know who wrote it (shockingly, that

11

happens a lot) or can't express his thoughts about it, he suspects the actor isn't deeply conscientious or commited to his or her work. After all, if you haven't taken the interest to research your own piece, it doesn't say much for how deeply you'll explore a play somebody else casts you in. It leaves the listener with the distinct impression of a casual superficiality towards the work—not the trait you want to be remembered for.

Which is where this book comes in. In the hope that you'll want to read the original play from which a *One on One* monologue you like was extracted, I've offered you some background about each of the plays in question.

If you take casting directors Simon and Carrig seriously, you'll eventually have to figure out what engages *you* about the entire play you've chosen. They'll want to know what's going through your mind.

You'll notice another thing: there are some pieces here that probably don't fit you—you're probably hovering in your twenties or thirties and auditioning for parts of that age. I've included a few pieces for actors as old as seventy (Pinter's *Party Time,* in the female version of *One on One*), Irish (*Dancing at Lughnasa*), and even hermaphrodites. The reason is that I enjoy these monologues as pieces of writing. They may not be all that useful to you as audition pieces, but they may just make your life a little fuller, a little better for having just read them. Or you might just learn them anyway to sharpen certain skills of acting and speaking. But Meg Simon warns that if you choose to do *Dancing at Lughnasa*, say, make sure you do the Irish accent; otherwise she'll assume you can't.

What's the piece for actors who are hermaphrodites? *Red Scare on Sunset* by Charles Busch in which Busch himself played the part of Mary Dale, who is very much a lady. See where you fit into that one! (I decided to put it into the *female* version of the book.)

I've included Harold Pinter's *Party Time* for its excellence, but the *female* monologue from it is in for another reason as well. It's spoken by a character who is seventy years old, and I hope some young actresses out there will give it a try. I'm tired of actors playing age by putting on tons of makeup and latex. That happens in the movies, of course. But you can actually "act" aging in the theater. The physical distance of your audience from you (and the aesthetic one, too) allows you to work without latex. What you need is practice. Pinter's play gives you ample opportunity.

Actually, what "fits" you as an actor is a tricky proposition. Conventional wisdom tells you to choose a monologue that suits you: if you're fat, don't play a gaunt; if you're a guy, don't play a doll; if you're young, don't play old, etc. Well, in 1972, I produced a play in a workshop at Lincoln Center called *Kool-Aid*. It was made up of two one-acts. One was set in a drug addict's apartment that served as a shooting gallery. Various addicts made their appearance and their speeches. One of these characters was a guy named Fat, who was just that.

I thought a friend of mine who had performed in an off-Broadway show was perfect for the role. When I offered it to him, he was offended because, "The only reason you want me for this role is that I'm fat." Actually, I thought of him for the part because he was funny and touching and a very good actor. When he turned me down, I suggested to the director an unknown actor I had seen in a movie, *Hi Mom!* That actor was funny and thin. But he never blinked when we asked him to audition.

His name was Robert DeNiro.

He read for the part and was very thin and very funny and he got the job.

Another play I produced, *El Grande de Coca-Cola*, needed a replacement actor, who at one point in the play would comically portray Toulouse-Lautrec. The tall Jeff Goldblum auditioned. A lot of the humor in that bit now came from the sight of Jeff playing the part on his knees—especially since Jeff on his knees is still about the same height as any normal person on his feet. He got laughs, not because he *couldn't* play Lautrec, but because he successfully "acted" small, giving the audience enough details of this dwarfish character that they could see beyond the lanky form on the stage. He, too, got the part he was after.

Most of the monologues in this book have been chosen with a generalized "you" in mind—the "you" that can be summed up by the age in parentheses on the contents page and the character descriptions accompanying the monologues. What people like Meg Simon and Randy Carrig are looking for in your audition is the *real* you, the individual spirit who can give a character life beyond written specifications in the script.

Here's how Ron Silver showed me *his* individuality. *El Grande de Coca-Cola* had become a big hit, in spite of the fact that it was mostly in Spanish (with some French and Italian and German, no English). We needed a replacement for the lead. The main requirement was that the actor be fluent in Spanish. Which meant that three quarters of those whom I interviewed tried to fake it with their year or two of high school Spanish.

The reason I was casting the replacement was that I had had a year or two of high school Spanish myself and could spot a fellow phoney a mile away.

After seeing two hundred actors, I decided the auditions were over and closed the door. A few minutes later, there was a terrible knocking. And this voice started to demand entry in a Spanish I couldn't understand. So, I figured he was a really bad faker and was determined to keep him out. Until he brayed in perfect English: "If I don't get this job, I'll have to go to _____."

He named a summer theater known as the Dachau of summer theaters, so abusive was it of its apprentices and non-Equity personnel.

Now, this shameless attempt at manipulation betrayed a real desperation on the actor's part. Something a lot of TV commercials and monologue books tell you is wrong to show—it's another of those sacred rules. But in this case, the individual who broke that rule succeeded in catching my attention—when I was supposed to have my mind on language skills—because I had been an apprentice at Dachau Summer Theater years before and knew exactly what the guy meant.

I opened the door and there stood Ron Silver. After several auditions (all in Spanish, which it turns out Ron can speak fluently) and a bizarre improvisation (in which Ron vividly performed a monologue about being born without a head, in Spanish), he got the part.

Another rule-breaker who managed to draw attention to himself was a friend of mine who one day decided to break the rule about dressing well for auditions. He had always done so, but he never got cast. One casting director used to pitch him into a vicious cycle of elation and dejection by repeatedly calling him in—and each time dismissing him by saying: "Sorry, this time it wasn't meant to be, but how glad I am that we finally had a chance to meet." As if she hadn't seen him fifteen times before!

My friend shrewdly figured out he wasn't making much of an impression. So, the next time he got the call, he went into the men's room before the interview and he doused himself with water until he looked like Gene Kelly in *Singin' in the Rain*. He ruined a good suit, too. But when he walked in the lady was dumbstruck. He didn't get that part, but a few days later she remembered him and called him about another part. And that was the start of a career that has gotten him parts in movies like *Wired*, *Big Business*, and *Barfly* and a home in Santa Barbara—which he leaves to take parts when he feels like it.

Finally, you'll notice that the title of this book is a basketball term. Basketball has its rules. But, as I have urged you to be skeptical about all the rules that editors prescribe, let me tell you this story about someone who broke what I have earlier referred to as a *very* important rule.

A famous actress asked me to read a movie script she had been given. She was being offered a lot of money. She watched me read it, gauged my reaction, and then asked whether her character was credibly written. When I said yes, she asked me to explain why. As we talked it over, I realized *she hadn't read the script!*

"Oh, I just read my part!" she admitted cheerfully.

After I insisted that she read the whole script, she met with the director, who disagreed with her feelings about everything in it. Now, she was upset and wondering whether she should have taken the part in the first place. But coincidentally the director was fired and the new one rewrote the entire script. The actress was brilliant in the movie and ran away with the reviews. And she probably never read the new script!

So what do I know?

Yes, basketball has rules. Monologue books? Forget it!

—JACK TEMCHIN

•Note: Brackets [   ] indicate that the speech is interrupted by another character in the original play. Most of these lines are well worth reading and thinking about as they will offer clues to the questions and issues which the main character is trying to answer.

•Note: If a monologue is too long for your audition or class, you may wish to judiciously cut the speech down to suit your purposes. While thinking about what can be cut from a speech, you'll also discover what's most important to the character and the dramatic moment. Whenever you do offer a cut version of any speech, you owe it to your audience to tell them so.

ADVICE FROM A CATERPILLAR by Douglas Carter Beane

SUIT, an investment banker, in his late thirties, waspy and conservative, plays a board game called Candyland with a gay East Village performance artist. Suit is married with a daughter, Lizbeth. And he's cheating on his wife.

SCENE: A country house in Old Chatham, New York.

TIME: The present.

SUIT: It's been a while since you played hasn't it? [SPAZ: Does it show?] You're headed for the molasses swamp. [SPAZ: Straight men and sports. I'm just not prepared.] I'm used to playing with Lizbeth. [SPAZ: How is she to play with?] She cheats. [(*SPAZ smiles.*)] You're thinking "Like father, like daughter" right? [SPAZ: Am I that obvious?] Pretty much. [SPAZ: Thank you. Lose one turn.] I don't really like it when she cheats. You know? She—uhm...I would like her to be above that. Not like—I don't mean to make it sound like I want her to be better than me. I mean my life is free. Secure. I'm proud of my solidness. Not that I'm insensitive to others when they're unsolid. I mean, I've had my moments of fragility, I guess. Back in my—God, must have been sophomore year of college—Jesus, I was out there. Very erratic. Met this girl, her name was...don't even remember. Beautiful. Looked like Cheryl Tiegs. I was a mess. Just, as I said, out there. Couldn't think of anything but being with her and drinking thick red wine and making love and writing awful poems that rhymed and...what was her name? My grades were in the basement. My dad—oh God—embarrassing memory—My dad had to come down and give me one of those your-mother-and-I lectures. "Your mother and I." (*He laughs.*) God. I used to get those speeches semi-annually like reports. But this time my old man seemed—I don't know—pretty fragile himself. Couldn't look me in the eye. And Dad

17

was big on eye contact. I could make eye contact before I could walk. So I broke up with the girl whose name I can't remember but who apparently was so important at the time. What can I tell you? I'm not one of those people who carry on like a French singer, right? "Life is to be lived on the edge, ho ho." [SPAZ: Hate them.] (*SUIT stops playing, SPAZ continues.*) Just doesn't appeal to me. I don't really think life needs to be so fragile. Just...keep it fine. Let's calm down and make money and let that be that. Not that I'm only a capitalist. I give back. I give back to the world. I give to the homeless and I give to cure AIDS and I give to the...the... [SPAZ: The what?] The other one. (*They both think for a moment, then:*) [SPAZ: The environment.] Right. The environment. So that Lizbeth can have things...solid. With a good foundation. (*Pause.*) And other people, too. (*Pause.*) Solid and grounded and secure and (*Pause. He smiles.*) Loretta. Loretta something. (*Pause. The smile fades.*) And safe and fine.

THE AMERICAN PLAN by Richard Greenberg

NICK LOCKRIDGE, a young wasp in his early twenties, has courted Lili Adler, the quiet, reclusive daughter of the sharp-tongued, German-Jewish refugee, Eva. Lili who initially is surprised at Nick's attentions ultimately falls in love with him. A wedding is planned. But her mother has caught Nick in several lies. Principally that his father died in a shooting accident. She accuses him of seeking Lili's fortune.

SCENE: Outside the Adlers' summer house in the Catskills.

TIME: Early 1960's.

NICK: After my mother died, my father more-or-less lost control of things. Not badly—it was more a kind of slip of attention. But, apparently, that's all it took. Things fell apart. It had something to do with a partner, I think, or the board—something shifty—I'm not suppressing the details here, I just never quite learned them. Anyway, just like that, it seemed, we were out of business. Suddenly, as you said. And, yes, broke. I was working in New York then, I'd visit on weekends. Every time I did, he'd have sold off another room of furniture and he'd be sitting in it...singing. "I'm a ramblin' wreck from Georgia Tech/And a heck of an engineer..." And he wasn't even drinking—that was the funny part, he was stone-cold sober. I'd say, "Dad...are you sure you're all right? Can I get you anything?" He'd say, "Oh, no, I'm fine, pal, I'm fine, sport—all I need is a shave and a haircut—that's all I need, sport—a shave and a haircut—just a shave and a haircut—then I'll be ready." (*Beat.*) He didn't understand how everything had happened to him so fast. He wasn't crazy, I don't think...just surprised...He started singing in the street. He'd forget to *bathe*. The house started looking like a junkheap. One day this group of men—five of them, I think...our neighbors...came to call on him. They said to him, "Nick, we're sorry to have to say this, but it doesn't look as if you're ever going to be able to take control of things. Wouldn't it be better to go, now, before you have to? Wouldn't it be better just to leave?" (*Beat.*) He called me in the city after. I said, "Oh, look, they're your friends, they'll forget about it." He said, "No...I stank up the street. You can do a lot of things, but you don't stink up the street." And he started to laugh. We hung up, he walked into his room...and had the unfortunate accident while cleaning his gun. (*Beat.*) I didn't tell any of this to Lili because, well, it isn't the sort of thing you say right at first...and because it was so pleasant not to. Those are the only reasons. (*Beat.*) Well. This has been a marvelous party, you've been a perfect hostess, and I've had a splendid time. (*Beat.*) I wish you would let me tell Lili instead of you.

AMERICAN WELCOME by Brian Friel

An AMERICAN director, in his late twenties, greets the great British dramatist whose play is about to start rehearsals.

SCENE: A hotel lobby.

TIME: The present.

A hotel lobby. Piped music in background.
Two chairs, one on each side of a small table. On one chair sits

19

the EUROPEAN, a large brown envelope on his lap. He casually surveys his surroundings.

After a few seconds the AMERICAN enters, carrying a brief case. He looks around, spots the EUROPEAN, bears down on him. The AMERICAN is young. He speaks very rapidly and gives excessive emphasis to several words in each sentence.

AMERICAN: It *is* Mr. Smith, isn't it? Mr. John Smith? I'd recognize that distinguished head anywhere! I'm Bert—remember? We've corresponded. I'm directing your play. Welcome, sir! Welcome to America!

(They shake hands.)

No-no. Don't get up—please. *(He sits.)* May I? Well! You've made it! You're here! Gosh! And may I tell you, sir, how honored and how privileged we are to have you here with us.

I'm sure you're still groggy with jet lag, are you? Can I get you something to eat, something to drink? How's your hotel? Had you a good flight? Can I get you a coffee? Tea? Beer? May I call you Joe? Thank you. And may I make a personal comment? You look so European—it's uncanny! *(Without breaking his speech he opens his briefcase and takes out a script and a large note-block.)* Wonderful. Okay. Let's get down to business. But before we do, Jim, may I tell you just once more how magnificent, how truly magnificent your play is—I mean that—and how honored and privileged I am to be associated with it. I really mean that. You see, Bill, what you have given us is a perfectly conceived and perfectly executed analysis of the human condition the world over. It's so perfect it—it—it's frightening. Beautiful form. Electrifying language. Subtle wit. Penetrating insights. I mean to say that's art—that's real art—that's European art, if you know what I mean. What I'm trying to say, Tom, is this: you have entrusted me with this delicate perfection—and I'm scared. I say to myself: Bert, can you handle it? Are you worthy of it?

You're tired. Can I get you something? Coffee? Tea? Beer?

Okay. Fine. What have I got here? A few questions. Do you mind if I ask you a few silly questions? Just for my own enlightenment. I knew you wouldn't mind. And may I tell you, Chuck, how honored and how privileged we are to have you here with us? First problem:

language. Frankly we're uneasy with the language. I mean to say we're not uneasy with the language—it's just that there's a lot of it we don't understand. Simply a question of usage: or to be more accurate, simply a question of our ignorance of your usage. I've made a list here—words like "boot," "bumper," "chemist"—there are maybe a dozen of them. Frankly we don't know what you mean. And since you want to communicate with American audiences and since we want them to understand you, I mean to say what we did was this. We went to our most distinguished American playwright—and you've got to meet him while you're here; he just adores your work—and what he did for us was this. He took all those little confusing words—five or six thousand approximately—and with wonderful delicacy and skill and with the utmost respect for the rhythms and tones of your speech, he did this most beautiful job of translating the play into the language we speak and understand. I hope you'll approve. I know you'll approve.

Can I get you something? Coffee? Tea? Beer? Gosh! I really can't believe it, Mike! You're actually here! I'm just knocked-out!

Okay. Second problem: the form of your play. We're uneasy with the form. I mean to say we're not uneasy with the form—it's just that you've written this wonderful naturalistic play but you've written it in monologue form! A naturalistic play in monologue form, for God's sake! I mean to say a monologue is just not naturalistic if you don't mind my saying so. Let me qualify that instantly. The monologue may be naturalistic in Europe but it is not "natural" to us. We talk, we exchange, we communicate. And since you want to communicate with American audiences and since we want them to understand you, I mean to say what we did was this. We went to our most distinguished American playwright—and you've got to meet him while you're here; he just reveres your work—and what he did for us was this. He took your little monologue and with wonderful delicacy and skill and with the utmost respect for the rhythms and tones of your speech, he did this most beautiful job of transforming your script into a four-character, two-act, single-set comedy that is just—how can I tell you?—just breathtaking. I hope you'll approve. I know you'll approve.

You're suffering from jet-lag—I can see it. Can I get you something? Gin? Whisky? Brandy? Gosh! I really can't believe it, Dan! You're actually here! I'm just knocked-out! (*He sits back,*

21

relaxes, smiles contentedly.) Well, that wasn't too bad now, was it? And here we are, all set to go. And let me tell you this. We think— hell, we know!—that we've got the most distinguished, the funniest, the most sensitive, the most disturbing, the most enlightening and the most moving play of the season—a big, big, big hit that is going to make us all rich and famous.

And may I tell you once more how honored and how privileged we are to have you here with us. May I shake that distinguished hand again?

Welcome, Tony Brown, welcome to America! (*He takes the EUROPEAN's hand and pumps it with enthusiasm.*)

ANTIGONE IN NEW YORK by Janusz Glowacki

Homeless people in lower New York try to retrieve the body of their friend Paulie and give him a decent burial. FLEA, thirties, a Pole, is a wheeler dealer, who knows how to succeed in America. Another immigrant has declared his intention of returning to Russia. Flea is swigging from a bottle.

SCENE: Tompkins Square Park.

TIME: The present.

FLEA: You know what? You're right. You should go back to Russia where you belong because you'll never make it here. I would never leave New York myself, not for nothing. They couldn't drag me away from this place. (*takes a sip*) Because I know how to live in America. I read the papers, keep up, and I know exactly what to do. When I hit the bottom then I will quietly walk to one of these fancy detox centers. Look at Larry Fortensky. He's as Polish as me. He liked to have a drink and now the whole world admires him. If he didn't drink who would he be? No one would have heard of him. He would be in the construction business, painting apartments. And look what happened to him. He was drinking like a good Pole and then he slowly floated to the bottom. Maybe he had a little delirium or a little epilepsy. Anyway, he went to a very elegant detox center and who is detoxing in the next room? Elizabeth Taylor and look. From one day to the next Fortensky's lying in a hammock just rocking back and forth, birds are singing, palms are waving, Michael Jackson is dancing around, some turtles, snakes, maybe some cats. Who the fuck knows? And Liz Taylor is tiptoeing around bringing him Wiborova with grapefruit juice. Because the most important thing in life is to be yourself.

ASSASSINS book by John Weidman, songs by Stephen Sondheim

SAM BYCK, mid-thirties, dictates one of his many letters to Leonard Bernstein.

SCENE: A park bench.

TIME: Christmas, 1973.

A park bench. SAM BYCK trudges on, wearing his Santa Claus suit, carrying his picket sign and a beat-up shopping bag. He sits down, reaches in the shopping bag, takes out a can of Yoo-Hoo, opens it, and takes a big drink. He then takes out a greasy sandwich, a portable tape recorder and a bunch of tapes. He shoves a tape in the tape recorder, takes a bite of sandwich, composes himself and starts recording.

BYCK: Hello, Mr. Bernstein? Lenny? How you doin'? My name is Sam Byck. We've never met. You're a world-renowned composer and conductor who travels the world over enjoying one success after another and I'm an out-of-work tire salesman, so I guess that's not surprising. But I hope you'll take a few minutes out of your busy schedule to listen to this tape which you just opened in the mail. If you can't listen to it now, maybe you can listen to it— (*He sings.*)

Tonight, tonight...

(*He chuckles cheerfully*) I love that song. What a melody! And what a sentiment. "Tonight, tonight, I'll meet my love tonight..." Where is she, Lenny? Gimme a hint. (*He takes a drink of Yoo-Hoo and a big bite of the sandwich*) Lenny, you're a modest kind of guy, I know that. But you'll indulge me for a minute if I say something from the heart. You're a genius. Yes, you are! And you know why? You understand what people want. You have their ear. You make 'em

23

listen, Lenny. No one listens. Are you listening?! No one listens... (*He takes anther bite of sandwich*) Well, if you're hearing this, I guess you're listening now, right? So with all due respect, deferring to your stature in the world of music, classical and semi-classical, I want to offer you a small piece of advice...Hey, I know what you're thinking. Who the hell is Sam Byck with his fat ass and his tongue on rye to give a shit hot guy such as yourself advice? Well, Lenny, it's a fact that my unwillingness to compromise my principles and kiss ass like some people I could mention has cost me the so-called good life which others have enjoyed. So be it, Len. Fuck me, fuck you. But Lenny, listen. Listen to one small piece of advice from a true fan... Forget the long-hair shit and write what you write best. *Love songs*. They're what we need! They're what the world needs! "Lonely Town!" "Maria!" Tender melodies to cherish for a lifetime! Timeless strains which linger in the memory and the heart! Love, Lenny! What the world needs now is love sweet love! Love makes the world go round! (*He takes a slurp of Yoo-Hoo*) Well, not exactly. Bullshit makes the world go round. You know that all too well, a worldly guy such as yourself. You know the world's a vicious, stinking pit of emptiness and pain. But not for long. I'm gonna change things, Lenny. I'm gonna drop a 747 on the White House and incinerate Dick Nixon. It's gonna make the news. You're gonna hear about it and I know what you're gonna ask yourself: What kind of world is this where a decent, stand-up guy like Sam Byck has to crash a plane into the President to make a point? You're gonna wonder if you want to go on living in a world like that. Well, lemme tell you, Len. You do. And you know why? So you can keep on writing love songs! Yes! There's a gorgeous world out there, a world of unicorns and waterfalls and puppy dogs! And you can save it! Through the medium of your God-given talent! *Do it*, Lenny! Save the world! Is that too much to ask?!...Oh, Lenny. One more thing. When you hear about my death you're gonna wonder if there's something more you could've done. Lenny, you did everything you could... (*He clicks off the tape recorder. A beat. Then he clicks it on again*) Well, maybe not *everything*. Maybe not absolutely everything, you know? Maybe one day you could've picked a phone up. Just picked up a phone and said, "Hey, Sammy, how's it going? Hang in there, Sam. This Bud's for you." How long would that have taken you? A minute?

Half a minute? That was too much, wasn't it? You probably had your limo double parked. You and your shit hot buddies had a plane to catch to Paris, France for dinner and a blow job. Hey, I understand. I undersand too well, my friend. You're just like all the rest of them— (*He flips through the tapes, reading names*) Jonas Salk, Jack Anderson, Hank Aaron... You knew where I was. You *all* did. And you know what you did? You left me there! You jerks! You shits! You pricks! You had your chance and now it's too damn late! Fuck me?! Fuck you! I'm outta here! I'm history, Lenny! Understand?! I'm history! (*He takes a big bite of his sandwich, chews. Lights fade, as he starts to sing...*)

> I like to be in America,
> O.K. by me in America,
> Knobs on the doors in America,
> Wall-to-wall floors in America!

(*Blackout*)

THE BALCONY SCENE by Wil Calhoun

ALVIN, in his thirties, repressed and afraid to leave his apartment, writes articles on American history. He has been falling in love with his new neighbor, Karen, who works in advertising. Here, he describes an attempt to go outside, which ends with Karen coming to the rescue.

SCENE: The balcony of ALVIN's apartment in Chicago.

TIME: The present.

ALVIN: Remember when I told you I wasn't crazy? [KAREN: I remember.] Well, I was wrong. I think I am crazy. [KAREN: Tell me what happened.] Well. When I left I was fine. I felt fine. Then I got about halfway down the block and I lit a cigarette. There was this old woman coming the other way and she asked me for a cigarette. Only she called it a "cigawette." She said, "Got a cigawette?" I had one lit and the pack was in my hand. I couldn't just keep walking. So, I shook

25

one out and it fell on the sidewalk and I didn't know if I should just give her that one so I shook another out and she took that one and bent down and took the other one from the sidewalk and put it in her pocket. Then she put the other one in her mouth and stood there for me to light it for her. So, I lit it, like she was my goddam girlfriend or something and she just walked away. Didn't say thank you or anything. Just walked away. (*ALVIN stops and looks at KAREN for some reaction. KAREN just looks at him. He continues.*) Well. I got to the video store and there must have been three hundred people in that place. Saturday. I forgot what Saturdays are like. I started looking around for the movies and it seemed like everywhere I went ten people followed right behind me. It was like we were all looking for the same movies. I couldn't get away. All of a sudden, I notice this kid standing in front of me. And he's staring at me. He's probably six or seven and he's got these glasses that have magnified his eyes about three times the normal size and he's just staring at me. He's filthy and there was stuff stuck all over his glasses. Looked like dried eggs and crumbs and God knows what else. The kid had his breakfast all over his glasses and he just kept staring at me. So I tried to get the hell away from him. I started getting really sweaty and itchy from all the people in the store and I had a hard time getting my breath. I just had to get out. Then, you know, I left but there was all those...I saw all those people in the street...cars and...I just knew I couldn't make it back by myself. That's when I called you.

THE BELLEVUE OF THE WEST SIDE by Leonard Melfi

Twenty-five people caught up in the bustle of Port Authority Bus Terminal all reach for rather than take from one another.

JESUS HAVANA, mid-twenties, Cuban American but could be almost any heritage. Handsome, charming, and full of energy, he practicallly lives at the Port Authority, where he sells fresh fruit from his vending cart. He also tends bar in one of the terminal's five bars.

SCENE: Port Authority Bus Terminal, New York City.

JESUS: I've been in love once...I mean really in love...the kind of love that happens only once in a lifetime, only once in a blue moon...there's always one out there for all of us...we don't realize that...but it's true...and this woman—she was a girl then—was the one and only one for me, yours truly here: Jesus Havana...her name was Dorothy Jean, and Dorothy Jean was like a pink candle that you knew would never go out...and this pink candle that was my Dorothy Jean not only burned beautifully all of the time, but she also gave off the smell of sweet perfume...it came from her flame, which never flickered, by the way: it was always a steady reaffirming sort of warm, lovely flame...no flickering ever!...no going out ever!...it was bright and constant, and she, Dorothy Jean, the pink candle, well, she gave off the scent of pink roses, the odor of pink carnations, the aroma of some mysterious pink flower that nobody knows the name of...my Dorothy Jean loved to live on the beach in the beautiful sunshine, but she also loved to stay inside on dark cold nights where she would sit in her room and where she would read all of the great love stories that were written over a hundred years ago...and we went dancing and swimming together...and we went to plays, and the opera, and to concerts, and to the ballet...and the first time we made love was in a high, high, high all-glassed-in-enclosed penthouse while down below us—as we watched from the bed—we witnessed the glittering array of breathtaking Manhattan during the pink heart of a cool breezy springtime with pinkish flowers and breathing bursting buds swaying and singing and softly sighing everywhere, no matter what, amid all those lights and all those buildings: nothing could stop God and Nature, so she thought, and so I thought...but then one day, one unforgettable, one unforgivable day something happened in the life of my Dorothy Jean: the house that she lived in, with her mother and her father and her younger brother and her younger sister and their dog Bark and their cat Meow, their house caught on fire because of electrical wiring, because everything was turned on at the same time, everything like three television sets, a computer, a microwave oven, the dishwasher, the food freezers in the cellar—I'm leaving some things out because I can't remember too much about it anymore—all these on all at the same time in their house, while Dorothy Jean sat upstairs in her lovely ivory tower bedroom reading or maybe even re-reading one of the great love stories written over a hundred years ago: reading it by candlelight, no less...and I would like to think that she was thinking about me, too, upstairs in her candle-lit bedroom...(*A pause, a long one*)...the house burned down to the ground...and there were no survivors: only...Dorothy Jean...and when she knew that she was the only member left of the family, she took off all of her clothes, and then she walked down the flagstone stairs that led to the sandy beach and wild roaring ocean...and then, very softly, very steadily: she slowly walked into the beckoning waves of the pounding blue sea...and then, just like that, before anyone knew it: she was gone!...swallowed up by the hypnotic sea...my Dorothy Jean!...snuffing out her own pink candle forever from this earth. (*Finally.*) I have been insane ever since.

THE BELLEVUE OF THE WEST SIDE by Leonard Melfi

Twenty-five people caught up in the bustle of Port Authority Bus Terminal all reach for rather than take from one another.

NICKY NUDIE, a handsome young guy in his early twenties, born and raised in New York City, is trying to forget some of the "porn" he did for a living a few years back. As he works at a newspaper stand he keeps his eye out for the right girl whom he can fall in love with and marry.

SCENE: Port Authority Bus Terminal, New York City.

TIME: The present.

NICKY: She disappeared on me. And I let her do it. It was the dumbest thing that I ever let happen to me. She was like a this out-of-town mouse visiting the Big Apple. The most beautiful mouse you ever did see, Zachary. She made my heart start tickling. My tongue, too. My pubic hairs were soaking wet when I got home last night. I almost didn't want to take a shower ever again. My dick was hard, then limp, then hard, then limp: it didn't know what it wanted to be. I guess it was happy and sad at the same time. The way I am right now. I hate when I feel like this. Actually, I've never felt like this before. This is really something new for me. It's torture. I could die right now. I didn't sleep last night hardly at all. Maybe two hours. All I could think of was this out-of-town mouse buying a paper from me yesterday afternoon. She was perfect. Young and pale-like and precious-looking like some doll. A sexy doll. A very sexy doll. I don't know what to do, Zachary. It's too much for me, too much to handle. In the last twenty-four hours everybody I've come in contact with thinks I'm a pain in the ass. I know they do. But I don't care. I've got to find her, if it's the last thing I do. (*A pause.*) I wacked-off last night to her. Three times. I guess that's why I only got two hours of sleep. One time I splashed against my bedroom window. It was the first time. I thought I broke it, the window. And then I dreamed about it: wacking off, splashing up against my bedroom window. In the dream the window was broken. I was glad it wasn't when I woke up. Or was I glad? Maybe not. I would love to have broken the window while I was awake as long as it had to do with her. I'm sick, Zachary.

BIG AL by Bryan Goluboff

LEO, twenty-eight, holding a machine gun, describes to his friend Ricky his bitter disappointment with Big Al.

SCENE: A downtown studio apartment, filled with Al Pacino memorabilia.

TIME: The present. Late night.

LEO: Just listen to me, O.K.? You know I've been writing him the last two years, letters, ideas, sent him my journals, I wanted him to learn everything about me. I bought all this stuff at auctions. You remember that, right? (*He holds up his machine gun.*) This is the machine gun from *Scarface*. I paid $200 for it. (*He pulls out a suitcase from under the bed filled with paraphernalia. He takes out a Police Cap.*) The Police Cap he wore in *Serpico*. $120. Hundreds of dollars in postage. You don't understand, Ricky…Never a reply. Nothing. When he was doing *Julius Caesar* at the Public, I went down to see him. I wanted an answer. I couldn't get a ticket. I had to imagine his performance. I waited outside the theatre for four and a half hours, until he came out, but I couldn't say anything. I was furious. I jumped in a cab and I followed him home, all the way up the west side. I saw his apartment building, everything. He got outta the cab. I was so mad, I was gonna do something. I wanted to be recognized, you know, I wanted to alter the course of his life, but something stopped me...Today, when my mailbox was empty, I said, "Fuck this life, man." I mean, where do you turn when your heroes let you down? [RICKY: He's just an actor, Leo—] Al Pacino talked to me from the screen. Why wouldn't he answer my letters?

BIG AL by Bryan Goluboff

LEO, twenty-eight, has summoned his writing partner, Ricky, in the middle of the night to tell him that they have a chance to write a script for Al Pacino.

SCENE: A downtown studio apartment, filled with Al Pacino memorabilia.

TIME: The present. Late night.

LEO: Ricky, I think about it a lot— [RICKY: What?] What it would be like to work with Al. You know, like we meet in pre-production and there's just this connection like boom! We get along right away because he's read my diaries. He knows how my mind works. And he loves my writing because it's real, it's connected to real things...Ah...I imagine he's gotta be really muscular for the role and me and him go to the gym and work out together. He looks in my eyes and he sees the same...I don't know, like I feel he's troubled, Rick, and I'm, I haven't been doing so well myself. He just takes me under. Maybe the *Times* does a story on the movie and there's a picture of me and Al in like black tank tops, just, he's got his hand like this— (*LEO grabs RICKY around the head and stares at him tensely.*) The caption would say, "Young screenwriter Leo Finn and Al Pacino share an intense moment on the set of *Maniac Priest*" or whatever the title is. Just shit I think about sometimes. Have an egg roll...

THE BIG FUNK by John Patrick Shanley

AUSTIN, a man in his twenties, introduces himself.

SCENE: East Village.

TIME: The present.

AUSTIN: Hi. My name's Austin. I believe in live and let live. I swear to God nobody believes in this but me. I'm in my house. I'm doin what I do when I'm not doin what I do. I'm an actor. And people come around, call, people try to get me to go here, do this, believe that, eat this, change my hair, change my clothes, my manners, my posture. I'll tell you this: It don't make me feel loved. And this is a battle. Cause people wanna tell you what to do. And they're looking for an angle, any angle, a way in. If they find out maybe you're a little shaky about your nose, then they'll talk about your nose all the time. How's your nose today? How do you feel about your nose? You must be upset about your nose. What are you gonna do about your nose? Until you scream in their face and tell 'em to get outta your business. Or you get a nose job. And if you do that, then they got you. This one part a you's not you anymore. It's somebody else's idea of how you should be. You're on your way to becoming somebody you don't know. A doll in dress-up clothes. I hate this fuckin society I wanna burn it down! But what? No. I don't. But sometimes I feel like it's me or them, me or society. I believe in live and let live, but society don't. You think we live in a time where everybody does what they want? You are wrong! I am not an anarchist fuck you truly. You should talk to me. Somebody should be talking to me. Cause in me and people like me I do believe lies a better world. We don't know how to make it better anymore than anybody else. But I'll tell you the main thing about me that makes what I just said so. I am a constructive person. (*Goes down into the audience.*) A constructive person. What's that?

Maybe it's a hero waitin to happen. But there are no job listings in the paper under hero. Heroes often go their whole lives unemployed. And in a way, that's what I hope happens. Because what if I'm wrong and I'm not a hero? I've never been tested. If I'm not tested, my tombstone should be carved into the shape of a big question mark. We could do something. I don't wanna settle. We could make things a lot better than they are. I know! You can explain why I'm wrong. Why the streets have to be dirty and the politicians have to be corrupt and drugs and starvation, and why there's cruelty right there in your face and you can't do anything about it. But you're wrong! Listen to me! I'm not wrong! We could make things better than they are. Living your life is supposed to make you weary. That's what death is for. Rest! You can't be lazy. You need to call up your guts. Cause it's just cowardice to say, Oh, that's the way things are. You can't do nothing about that. I'm telling you, Brothers and Sisters, we could be heroes!

BLACK EAGLES by Leslie Lee

An escort squadron of black flyers struggles against racism to win the right to fly their own missions in WWII.

LEON, in his twenties, relives the solidarity of his mates—the Black Eagles—in flight.

SCENE: Italy in the barracks of American flyers.

TIME: 1944.

The lights rise on YOUNG EAGLES who are in barracks, relaxing. THE ELDERS enter. Music can be heard behind them.

LEON: We were approaching the target at Anzio, and as usual, the German Gunners were blasting away—beautiful red and orange bursts of fire and smoke. Death, but still beautiful, sending huge hunks of flak, floating lazily up into the air, as if in slow motion, so slow it seemed that if you just reached out, it would slide gently into your hand. But it was a delusion. A volley of it slammed into my ship and tore my landing gear off. I heard another bang and when I looked back, my tail was coming apart. That lazy, floating, harmless fig kept slamming into me. I dropped down. In my seat behind the armored plates to protect myself. But just then, flak sliced through the door, like a knife through soft butter, and smacked into my leg. Jesus Christ, it hurt—hurt like I've never been hurt before. I called Nolan and I told him, "I'm hit, my ship's hit!" And he said, "Hold on, partner, hold on!" I kept dropping. I managed to clear the top of a mountain by only a couple of feet. And then, all of a sudden, I hear Nolan and Clarkie over the intercom, singing. (*Singing.*) "Swing low, sweet chariot, coming for to carry you home!" And two guys—you two, wild, crazy, beautiful, daring, adventurous fools, got on both sides of my ship, placed their wing tips under mine, lifted me, and flew me home! And that's what being a Black Eagle is all about.

BORN GUILTY by Ari Roth based on the book by Peter Sichrovsky

Peter, a Jewish journalist, the child of Holocaust survivors, interviews RUDOLF, an aging child of a Nazi officer. Rudolf's florid confession, his deep sense of victimization about growing up an exile in South America, suggests a kinship to his Jewish interrogator which prompts Peter to label Rudolf "The Guilty One."

SCENE: Rudolf's apartment in Germany.

TIME: 1986.

RUDOLF: Come, Peter. Enough questions. I want to ask one of you now. Do you ever get nightmares? You know the ones. Big? Black? Lacerating? What do you do with them? I've been to doctors, therapists, specialists: "Come to terms," they say. Yes, but whose? No terms exist, wouldn't you agree?

(*More or less like a bad performance*) Always at night, they come, tear me out of bed, push me into a car, men in uniforms. We stop at a house. I'm shoved down stairs into a room. A white room. I'm handed a towel and a cake of soap. They rip off my pajamas. Doors lock. I look up, I see them: Shower heads. And through the holes, a hisssssss... Fall to the floor. Soap cake turning to Zyklon.

Trouble breathing. Beginning to choke. Rush for the door, try to open it, bang on it, silent scream, eyes are burning. Fingernails. Excrement. Tractor ploughs. My parents eating cheesecake. I wake up. As soon as I close my eyes it starts again—shower heads, fingernails, cheesecake.

Well? What am I? Hero? Villain? Victim? Murderer? I think I'm a murderer, and do I get any congratulations for it, hmmm? What about you? You think I'm a fraud, don't you? Tell me, Peter. Does the name "Project Reinhard" ring a bell?...I thought it might. Can you imagine, growing up in South America surrounded by *Einzadst Reinhard!?* German schools, German book store, German tavern, German butcher, all in the middle of a jungle! All the money came from "Reinhard." Fake names. Fake passports. By the time I was ten, it had moved us four times. Then one day, they stopped looking for us, we were no longer dangerous. We were allowed to settle into a nice little villa, surrounded by nice little slaves—I can't tell you where exactly, it's too horrible, how we ruined them; Oh, those poor little brown people. Overnight, we had become victors. Eternal spring, fertile soil. Is this more what you'd like to hear?

A paradise, that's what it was. But I was fat. A real officer's kid. "Why was I born?" Hmmm? Have you ever asked yourself? Where did our parents get the insane notion to make a child? This was the question asked by Jodl after he was sentenced to death at Nuremberg. Quite a question. Tea?

I've read everything from that trial, eight thousand pages. Of all the defendants, Hans Frank I believe is the only one to have voiced any regret. I often try to imagine what father would have said. "What's all the excitement about?" *He* didn't do anything. "Driving into a village? Rounding up some Poles? Walk to a clearing, men here, women there. Men dig a trench and the women pile their clothes?" Once, one single time, my father was drunk enough to talk about it, how terrible it had been, that time they had to shoot the children one by one with a hand-gun because those idiotic soldiers had aimed their rifles too high. "Oh my God!" he sobbed! "What bad times those were!" How he loved to whine... In his will he requested to be buried in Germany, but I prevented it. No more orders. He used to whip me repeatedly for even the slightest provocation. I remember once, he discovered some money missing. Not much. He used to throw change in a bowl for tips and now it was gone. Well, he decided he was going to show US who was Boss! So one night he called in The Slaves. One by one, he told them they had "one hour to report the culprit or they'd all be fired!" I was twelve at the time. Slowly, I raised my hand. I suggested that maybe dear papa might be mistaken: Perhaps it was *I* who had taken the money...! Father turned bright red. He sent them out, all the while cursing them, "HOW DARE YOU? HOW DARE YOU?" And you know why he was so upset? Because I'd said it in SPANISH. *"Dejelos solos; Yo lo hice; Yo fui el que tome el dinero!"* I'd humiliated him in front of The Help! My first puny triumph.

By the time I was fifteen, I had gotten quite good at it. I'd lost twenty pounds. Suddenly I had a lot of friends. I would hitch-hike into town, I could have anyone I wanted. Back then, of course. You know what mother said? "Twenty years ago they would have pinned a pink triangle on you!" My father, he just wanted to kill me, or maybe himself first, then me. It was all over for German honor, that's for sure. No more beer in the taverns. No more chairman of the annual carnival committee. They crawled into their shells. Once I realized, I became completely uninhibited. I brought friends over, left magazines under the bed so they could find them. I dressed like a fag, talked like a fag, *"especially if a visitor ever came to the door!"* I really let 'em have it! You should have seen. I was kicked out of school for sexual molestation, it was beautiful! My father was called to the principal's office. I think it was the second worst day of his life! I am convinced that anything, even being charged with Crimes Against Humanity, would have been preferable. But his son A FAGGOT!?

You see, here's my theory: I think he drove into that tree on purpose. "Burned beyond recognition." That's what was written on the report. And it was gorgeous. Absolutely gorgeous. A fireball. An atomic blast. Unfortunately, I didn't see it. But *I was there.* The night after the funeral I went back to the cemetery and pissed on his grave, trampled on it, cried, went crazy. It was my own personal farewell. The next day, I waited for friends to call. Nothing. No cake. No congratulations. Did even one of those creeps tell me how much they admired me?

So I sold everything and came to Berlin. After all, I still had my German passport, and all the money I needed. I still don't have to work, and I don't. I don't work. I haven't done a thing in fifteen years except read about the Third Reich, and what's wrong with that, hmmm? Who reads anymore? Just us. Over and over I come across my father's name, his old one. I don't think I can mention it here. It stays with me—a deeply buried secret.

BY WHERE THE OLD SHED USED TO BE by Craig Warner

This English radio play is a very modern and dark retelling of Cinderella. Sarah, the youngest daughter in a formerly rich family now down on its luck, is treated viciously by her older sisters and mother. The punishment escalates when she is caught making love to a factory worker, named WILLIAM, also in his twenties. Sarah promises to return to William in the spring. Here, William tells his friend of his plans for Sarah's return.

SCENE: A pasture in an English village.

TIME: The present.

WILLIAM: This is the place we were. This is it. This is the place. Don't go any farther: her smell is on every tree. Look, patches of grass are missing where she pulled up clumps in her fist or jerked her head to the side and chewed it with her eyes shut hard. [FRANK: Sounds a bit dodgy on the ecology.] (*Leaves crackle under their feet as they roam.*) See that flat spot over there by the stream? [FRANK: Yeah.] There was a shed there, built by her father when she was a little girl. He built the shed for storage, but he kept it empty and he'd come up on warm evenings or during the day and take her with him, tell her fairy stories, hold her upside-down, whip her with daisies, and talk about what's at the centre of the earth. When he died he was burned by his wife and her two daughters, and that evening termites gobbled the shed till all that was left was the square in the grass where the shed used to be and one whipping-daisy curled up dead in the green. [FRANK: William, I...how can I say this? You've gone barmy. Loopy. Round the twist, off the deep end! Come with me. I know a girl who'll make you forget all about your—] No. She's coming here. (*A gust of wind.*) [FRANK: It's cold, William. What'll you *do* up here?] I'll keep myself

36

busy. I'll build a house for us to live in, where the shed used to be. I'll make the walls of plaited stems and peach skin and shreds of morning glory, the roof a mop of willow brushes, and a bed of dandelion dust. Inside I'll weave buttercups in the walls and in the bowls wedge fireflies for light. For blankets: sparrows' down stitched with spider webs. For curtains: lambs' wool dyed with African violets. The floor will be earth sprinkled with poppy seeds and one day in late spring she'll wake up with her belly swollen and orange, pink and blue poppies will be growing between her toes to catch the falling child and wrestle him, giggling, into this world.

CARBONDALE DREAMS by Steven Sater

The play describes a funny (to us) and disastrous (to them) reunion of the members of a Jewish family for Thanksgiving in the place they grew up, Carbondale, Illinois. Dominated by a mother who thinks only of food, each family member has found his own method of escape. One daughter is an overeater. A son, Bradley, is a cocaine addict. And DAVID, thirty, is a poet, who has geographically escaped to New York City.

DAVID: So I got this call from my Mother, right? Really. (*A beat. He speaks as his Mother.*) "Honey, don't come home for Thanksgiving." (*Now as himself.*) "What?" (*Now as his Mother.*) "Honey, don't come home. Don't come home to see *me*. So what if I die without seeing you? What's the big thing?" (*A beat.*) "Honey, don't come home to see your brother Bradley. God help him, David. Your talking won't change anything." (*A beat.*) "Baby, don't come home to see Beth, your poor sister. Oh, David, it goes beyond decency. You know I've tried everything. What is there left that another human being could say?" (*A beat.*) "David, don't come home to see your poor father. My husband! Who knew he'd turn out this way?" (*A beat.*) "No, David, come home so you can be happy." (*A beat. Now he speaks as himself.*) "But, Mom, if I want to be happy I'll stay here, okay?" (*A beat.*) And I slammed down the phone. An adult now; defiant. (*A beat.*) The next day I called up and booked my seat on the plane. (*A beat.*) I called my Mother. She said, "Oh, I'm so happy. Now I can go to my grave without being in pain." (*A beat.*)

So okay, I came home. My Mother had said to me, "Wait there for Bradley. Be a big brother. God knows your brother could use a big brother. Wait there for Bradley and talk to him, honey." (*A beat.*) I waited around in the airport two hours. I called Brad's machine. I kept thinking I saw him. (*A beat.*) Finally I went and called my Dad up. He said he was watching a golf match on TV. He'd be there as soon as it ended. What could I say? (*A beat.*) It's funny, you know, then when he picked me up, there we were, in the smell of his new car, and again I just couldn't find anything I could say. I mean, it was real hard, watching him wanting to tell me how sick he was. (*A beat.*) Finally he said, "You know, son, I know it's like going through hell for you, coming home. Coming back here where you always were sick and stuff. Still, you don't know what it means to your Mother." (*A beat.*) Meanwhile, I could see his hand was trembling; sitting on the steering wheel trembling like a mute white thing. (*A beat.*) Again I wanted to say something to him, but once again—I don't know—I couldn't quite speak. (*A beat.*) Finally he turned to me and said, "You know, son, I always thank God that I found golf." I said, "Huh?" (*A beat.*) He said, "I'll tell you, you don't know, swinging that golf club—it's like my own slice of eternity. Really, son." (*A beat.*)

CLAPTRAP by Ken Friedman

Sam and HARVEY, in their twenties, have been roommates in New York for two years. Sam is an aspiring novelist, playwright, and poet. Harvey is desperate to become an actor. When he comes back from an audition, Harvey begs Sam to ask him how his day has been. Sam obliges.

SCENE: Their fifth-floor walkup in Hell's Kitchen.

TIME: The present.

HARVEY: Ohhhhhh, I've screwed up a lot of auditions. I've done it all. Been late, caught in traffic, auditioned in a funeral parlor, you'll remember that one. But, today your roommate got stuck in an elevator. [SAM: (*laughing*) Stuck in an elevator? Really? Oh, isn't that too bad?] Can you believe it? Yes, at CBS! You see? You're laughing.

But, is it bad luck? To audition for a soap opera. [SAM: Gee, that's really some bad luck. (*SAM loves it.*)] No! It's the best luck! (*The trap is sprung.*) The best thing that's ever happened to me! Go on, ask, Sam! Ask me! [SAM: What are you talking about? Is there a lawsuit? You got a lawsuit! HARVEY: Better than a lawsuit.] Because do you know who was stuck on that elevator with me? Do you? I know. Jack Applebottom! [SAM: Jack who?] (*He's off and running.*) He's head of CBS Program Development East Coast. So, what do you do when you're stuck in an elevator? You pass the time. Jack Applebottom. Harvey Wheatcraft. Hello. Hello. "Well, Mr. Applebottom, looking for any new ideas?" He says, "For sitcoms? Always looking." I think fast. I say, "How about this? Two guys are roommates. One's a mediocre writer. The other a great actor. Both are struggling. The handsome one, the actor, gets to Broadway and becomes an overnight star, but out of the kindness in his heart and the pity he feels for his untalented roommate, he never tells him, so that the actor goes on living in the tenement, leading two separate lives: by night, the toast of Broadway; by day, just another failure like his roommate." What do you think? [SAM: Of that? It's ridiculous.] *He loved it! Yes! He loved it and he bought it! Thirty-five thousand dollars!* I'm rich. Aren't you happy for me? Aren't you glad? But, wait. There's more. We're still in the elevator. He says, "I'm also looking for a Movie of the Week." I'm cooking. I say, "Picture this, Jack...it's morning, a dozen people are going to work. People from all walks of life. The pregnant secretary, the alcoholic V.P. The madman with a bomb, the guy who's going to jump and what happens to them? *They get stuck in an elevator!* We'd call it *Elevator '87!*" He went nuts! The greatest idea he'd ever heard since he's been in T.V. He wants it. Forty-five thousand dollars. [SAM: You're making this up!] He said to me, "Have you ever written anything?" I said, "No." He said, "That's okay. Anybody can write." Aren't you happy for me? Aren't you thrilled inside? *It's true!* [SAM: I...I...] Wait. There's more. We got off the elevator. My heart is pounding. He says, "Kid, I'm also looking for a mini-series." "Hold it!...*Corridor!* The people behind the doors, in the closets, the intrigues, the loves, the hates, the passions that happen only in a hallway, starring who? The survivors of *Elevator!*" *He loved it!* Another hundred and twenty-five thou! We walk into his office.

"Wait! I've got the spin-off! *Office!* The lives of big business, small business as seen from the point of view of the cleaning lady, the curtains, and the furniture." He grabs me. He hugs me. He says, "Harvey, who's your agent?" Agent? Agent? I don't have an agent. [SAM: I'll represent you!] So, I make up a name, Barry Levy. [SAM: Barry Levy? A dumb name!] He knows him! Applebottom knows Levy. Barry Levy at William Morris. He gives me the phone. "Here, call Levy." I don't know what to do. So I dial. I say, "Let me talk with Barry Levy." The woman says, "There is no Barry Levy here." I say, "This is Harvey Wheatcraft and I just made four deals at CBS." *(becoming the woman)* "Barry. Barry Levy, pick up on five." Why not? If I can make up four shows they can make up one agent. Barry Levy gets on the phone. He doesn't know who I am, but so what? He doesn't know who he is either. I give him to Applebottom. They shmooze. They even reminisce. They make the deals. A total of...are you listening, Sam?...Two hundred sixty-five thousand dollars. Aren't you happy for me; deep inside aren't you pleased? I almost die. I can't believe it's actually happening to me. Applebottom says, "I have to call the coast for approval."

[SAM: Approval. If he doesn't get approval, what happens, Harvey?]

In show business, every deal always hangs on one more phone call. He has to talk to Burt White on the coast. He dials. My heart is pounding. My weak heart is beating like a drum. I'm scared to death. He gets through. [SAM: Yes? What happened?] Burt White has just been fired. *(HARVEY is crushed.)* Fired. [SAM: And all the deals fell through and you got nothing.] *(near collapse)* I...[I didn't know.] Jack asked, "Who's taking Burt White's place?"...Do you know?...*Jack Applebottom!* Yes! He has to approve his own deals! He gets on two phones. I still have a chance. Jack Applebottom East Coast is now Jack Applebottom West Coast. He has to talk to himself. More problems. Jack West Coast has no respect for Jack East Coast. He's made a lot of mistakes in the past. He only got the job through a relative. But Jack East Coast is fighting from strength. He says, "Dammit, if you don't approve these shows, I'm quitting!" Why not? He already has another job at higher pay!...He approves the deals. It's true. I've got them all. Two hundred sixty-five thousand dollars. Let me just say "Yes" one more time. Let it just sink in slowly. *Yes!!!* Isn't it ironic? Here you've been writing for years on the great American page One and you haven't made a dime, not a nickel, and I've been a writer for only fifteen minutes and I've made two hundred sixty-five thousand dollars!!! Aren't you happy for me, Sam? Aren't you thrilled that one of us finally made it and it was me!

CONVERSATIONS WITH MY FATHER by Herb Gardner

EDDIE GOLDBERG, in his early forties, is pugnacious, fiercely American, irascible, and chauvinistic. He speaks with a slight European accent which betrays his origins. He demands a lot even from his baby boy. He tries to bully his son into speaking his first words.

SCENE: A bar on Canal Street, New York City.

TIME: July 4, 1936.

EDDIE: (*He points to the Moose*) *Moose.* See? See the nice Moose? Moose, that's an easy one. An "M" at the beginning, "MMM," and then "OOOO"; Moose. Mmmmooose. See the pretty moose? Just look at the Moose. Moose.
(*He waits. Silence from the Stroller*)
Forget the moose. We'll wait on the Moose. "Duckie." Hey, how about duckie? You had duckie last Saturday, you had it down cold. Duckie.
(*Reaches under Stroller, takes out wooden duck, presents duck*)
Here ya go, here ya go; duckie. *Here's* the duckie. Look at that duckie; helluva duckie, hah? Hah?
(*Hides the duck behind his back*)
Where's the duckie? You want the duckie? Ask me for the duckie. Say "duckie."
(*Silence for a moment; he leans against the bar*)
You lost it. You lost "duckie." You had it and you lost it. Now we're losin' what we *had*, we're goin' *back*wards, Charlie.
(*Starts to pace in front of bar*)
Kid, you're gonna be two; we gotta get movin' here. Goddamn *two*, kid. I mean, your brother Joey—your age—we had a Goddamn

41

conver*sationalist* in there!

(*Silence for a moment*)

Charlie, Charlie, you got any idea how much heartache you're givin' us with this issue, with this Goddamn vow of *silence* here? Six words in two years and now *gornisht*, not even a "Mama" or a "Papa."

(*Grabs the batch of flags, starts placing one on each table about the room; quietly, controlling himself*)

Frankly, I'm concerned about your mother. Granted, the woman is not exactly a hundred percent in the Brains Department her*self*, also a little on the wacky side, also she don't hear a Goddamn word anybody says so why should you want to talk to her in the first place—nevertheless, on this issue, my heart goes out to the woman. She got a kid who don't do shit. She goes to Rutgers Square every morning with the other mothers, they sit on the long bench there—in every stroller, right down the line, we got talkin', we got singin' we got tricks; in *your* stroller we got *gornisht*. We got a kid who don't make an *effort*, a boy who don't *extend* himself.

(*Leaning down close to Stroller*)

That's the *trouble* with you, you don't *extend* yourself. You never *did*. You don't *now*, you never *did*, and you never *will*.

(*Suddenly, urgently, whispering*)

Come on, kid, gimme something, what's it *to* ya? I open for business in an hour, every morning the regulars come in, you *stare* at them; I tell 'em you're sick, I cover for you. It's July Fourth, a special occasion, be an American, make an effort.

(*Grabs the duck off the bar, leans down to the Stroller with it*)

Come on: "duckie," just a "duckie," one "duckie" would be a Mitzvah...

(*Silence form the Stroller; then the beginnings of a sound, barely audible at first; EDDIE leans forward, smiling hopefully*)

What's that? What...?

(*The sound grows louder, but there is no discernible word, and finally what we hear quite clearly is pure baby-babble, something like "ba-bap, ba-bap, ba-bap..."*)

Oh, shut up. Just *shut* up, will ya! If that's how you're gonna talk then shut ya Goddamn *trap*!

(*EDDIE turns sharply and throws the wooden duck violently across the room—it smashes against the farthest Down Right booth, barely missing Charlie who has been seated in the booth, watching—Charlie turns, startled, as the pieces of the duck clatter to the floor. EDDIE strides angrily over to the bar and then behind it, turning his back to the Stroller, starts to clean glasses from the sink and slap them onto a shelf as the baby-babble continues. He shouts)*

The conversation is *over*, kid!

(The baby-babble stops abruptly. Silence for a moment)

CONVERSATIONS WITH MY FATHER by Herb Gardner

JOEY GOLDBERG, a talented boxer of about seventeen, never shows for the big fight his family and friends expect him to win. When he finally returns, he explains his sudden decision to quit. Earlier that day, his father had read him the news that Jews in Europe were being rounded up and sent to their deaths.

SCENE: The Goldbergs' family bar on Canal Street, New York City.

TIME: 1944.

JOEY: *(Continuing, firmly)* This mornin', workin' out with Bimmy, we're skippin', we're sparrin', my mind ain't there, Pop. I'm doin' math. Three hundred and fifty thousand Jews in twenty-one days, comes out seventeen thousand, five hundred a day, *this* day, today—

[Eddie: A buncha crazy *stories*, Joey, I told ya—*(Wheeling on Zaretsky)* You, it's you and your Goddamn *bull*shit—]

(Moving towards him)

Please, ya gotta be quiet, Pop. That's maybe two thousand just while I'm workin' out. Seventeen thousand five hundred a day. No, it's impossible, I figure; Pop's *right*, it's nuts. I keep punchin' the bag. I come back to pick up Charlie, we're headin' over, not Seven yet; then I hear people hollerin', I look up, I see it. Top of The Forward Buildin', tallest damn buildin' around here, there's the "Jewish Daily Forward" sign, y'know, big, maybe thirty feet high and wide as the buildin', electric bulbs, ya can see it even deep into Brooklyn, *forever*, Pop. What they did is they took out the right bulbs, exactly the right bulbs, gotta be hundreds of 'em, so the sign says: "Jew Is For War";

it's Goddamn blazin' over the city, Pop, and Charlie and me start runnin' towards it, we're still maybe eight blocks away, we're passin' alotta people and kids on Canal, pointin' up, laughin', some cheerin', "Son of a *bitch*, son of a *bitch*, we fight the *war* and the Jews get *rich*," a guy grabs my arm, smilin', musta seen me box, guy my age, he says, "Pete, Pete, let's go get us some Yids, Pete!" and I know that second for sure they are doin' seventeen thousand five hundred a day, somewhere, seventeen thousand five hundred a day and I'm a guy spends his time boppin' kids for a silver-plated watch from Big Mike, hockable for fifteen dollars; right now I wouldn't hock me for a dime. Point is, I'm goin' in, Pop. I'm gettin' into this war and I need your help, now.

(*Eddie is silent*)

Army don't register me till next month, then it could be a year, more, before they call me. *Navy*, Pop, navy's the game; they take ya at seventeen with a parent's consent. Eight A.M. tomorrow I'm at Ninety Church, I pick up the Consent Form, you fill it out, sign it, ten days later Boot Camp at Lake Geneva, September I'm in it, Pop. Corvette, Destroyer, Sub chaser, whatever, *in* the Goddamn thing.

CREDO by Craig Lucas

A lone PERSON speaks.

SCENE: Uncertain.

TIME: Unknown.

(*Lights up. Person alone on stage.*)

PERSON:

So it's Christmas eve,
I go out with the dog.
Jim and I have just broken up.
I've just been to an AA meeting
Where a woman got up
And said she had no friends,

Her best friend is her VCR
And it's broken.
I came home to the hole where the sofa was.
There's no Christmas tree either.
I can't stand the thought of sweeping up all the dead needles
And dragging the carcass out to the street
To join all the other dead trees
With what's happening to the rain forest.
I know the two aren't connected,
But anyway, I pull up a folding chair
And heat up a piece of cold pizza.
This, I think, is the low point.
The walls show little ghosts where the pictures once were.
I go out.

Did I tell you I didn't get my Christmas bonus?
Well, I wasn't expecting it,
But I haven't been able to take Apple to the vet about her problem,
So she dribbles a little across the lobby,
Past the doorman who isn't smiling at me;
I'm sure it's because I haven't given him *his* Christmas bonus,
But maybe it's the trail of urine, too,
I don't stop to ask.
I smile bravely
And step outside where it has of course started to rain.
And people are running and looking very upset.
Surely the rain isn't that bad.
I turn:
There's been an accident on my corner.
I snap my head away,
I know if I look there'll be a baby carriage there
In the middle of the street.
I refuse to look.
They certainly don't need another person standing around, not doing
     anything.
I put my mind...Where can I put my mind?
Vienna.

Where Jim has gone with the woman he left me for.
You can't escape these thoughts.
All I know is her name.
Her name...is Carmella.
Apparently.
And I believe that she has had a sex change.
As far as I know, this has no basis in fact,
But I believe it as firmly as I believe
We are all headed straight to hell
If the Republicans spend one more minute
In the White House.

Where,
Where can I put my thoughts?
Ecuador.
My parents are in Ecuador.
They asked me to join them,
And I said
No, Jim and I would be spending the holiday together.
I hope that he and Carmella are caught
In the crossfire of some [terrorist]...
No, I don't.
Not really. But you know:
The sort of thing you see
On the evening news.
If you have a TV.
Or a phone.
Jim stopped paying the bills months ago,
As a kind of secret warning of what was to come.
But I refuse,
In my bones I refuse
To see myself as a victim.
I have gotten myself into this.
I allowed him to talk me into maintaining a joint bank account.
Every time a little voice in my head would say
Watch out.
He's cute,

But he's not that nice.
Beneath it all,
Behind the charm,
His chin,
That first night,
And then again in Barbados,
Beneath it all
Is *him*.
I alone took each and every step
Which brought me here
To this street corner
In the rain
On Christmas eve
With my dog whose urinary infection
I cannot afford to fix.
And at that moment, my friends,
My dog squats,
And the worst thing that has ever happened to me
Unfolds before my very eyes.
A wire, a loose plug from somebody's Christmas decorations
Carelessly strung in front of their little tea shop…
Electrocutes my dog.
And she falls immediately dead
On the sidewalk
In a sputter of sparks…
And the lights go out all down the front of the tea shop.
And a man comes out:
"What did you do?"
And I drop to my knees, unafraid,
Let me die, too,
Electrocute me.
And I embrace my dog, Apple,
Whom I have had for sixteen years.
She is my oldest friend.
She has seen me in my darkest, most drunken days.
She has been to every corner of my life, watched me make love.
She growled at the dogs on the dogfood commercials.

She has been across the country and back.
Apple, I'm not afraid to say, is the purest,
Most uncomplicated expression of love I have ever known.
And she has been killed by an electric current
In the last sick days of her valiant existence.

The man stares at me from above.
"Oh my god" he says.
He can't believe it
Any more than I can believe it.
Come in, he says.
We carry Apple into the shop.
To me she smells good,
But to some people she does not.
It's been too cold to bathe her.
It's hard for one person to hold her in the shower.
She doesn't like the water.

The man offers me the only thing he has.
Tea.
We talk,
And he assures me that the accident on the corner
Did *not* involve a child.
And no one was killed.

What to do now with Apple?
I can't cry anymore.
I have cried so much the last two weeks
I can't cry for her now.
And I know…
In some way I see all at once that
Jim was not really good enough for me,
That I will meet someone else.
And even if I don't I will have
An extraordinary and rich and complicated life.
It is entirely up to me.
I will most likely survive all the roadblocks and the detours.

As my dad always says:
"Life can be rough, but think about the alternative."

But then again
He's never been sick a day in his life.
He hasn't ever had to struggle just to stand
Or been unable to stop himself from peeing
Where he knows he shouldn't
And doesn't want to,
But there it is in a stream,
Surprising him and me.
He's never had to look up
With big sorrowful eyes which say:
"I had no idea.
I know this is wrong.
Don't yell."

No.
I only hope that I will go as quickly as Apple
When the time comes.
And if I don't,
I will absolutely,
I *know* I will face that bravely
And with dignity.
I know.
And if,
For some unforeseen but totally justified reason,
I can't,
And I am making a complete ass of myself,
Saying things I wouldn't ever say
And acting childishly
And turning into a prude
And a conservative
And am being a complete drag on everyone
For months and years,
I know my friends will forgive me.
And if for some equally valid and twisted,

But ultimately logical reason,
They don't,
Or they can't,
Or they're all dead by then,
Or it's August and they're away,
Then I will forgive them,
Right?
The same way I forgave myself
For yelling at Apple the first time she peed
Before I realized what was going on.

And if...
Again, if I can't,
And everything is entirely for shit
And I can't even find my way to the end of a sentence...
And...you can fill in all the blanks...

That will be fine, too.

DANCING AT LUGHNASA by Brian Friel

MICHAEL reminisces about the lives of his mother and her four sisters as they lived in 1936 in County Donegal, Ireland. Two of the aunts have left home only to die miserably later.

SCENE: The kitchen of their house, where the family spent all its time.

TIME: Lughnasa (loo-na-sa), the feast day of the Irish god Lugh at harvest time. 1956.

MICHAEL: But there is one memory of that Lughnasa time that visits me most often; and what fascinates me about that memory is that it owes nothing to fact. In that memory atmosphere is more real than incident and everything is simultaneously actual and illusory. In that memory, too, the air is nostalgic with the music of the thirties. It drifts in from somewhere far away—a mirage of sound—a dream music that is both heard and imagined; that seems to be both itself and its own echo; a sound so alluring and so mesmeric that the afternoon is bewitched, maybe haunted, by it. And what is so strange about that memory is that everybody seems to be floating on those sweet sounds, moving rhythmically, languorously, in complete isolation; responding more to the mood of the music than to its beat. When I remember it, I think of it as dancing. Dancing with eyes half closed because to open them would break the spell. Dancing as if language had surrendered to movement—as if this ritual, this wordless ceremony, was now the way to speak, to whisper private and sacred things, to be in touch with some otherness. Dancing as if the very heart of life and all its hopes might be found in those assuaging notes and those hushed rhythms and in those silent and hypnotic movements. Dancing as if language no longer existed because words were no longer necessary… (*Slowly bring up the music. Slowly bring down the lights.*)

DEARLY DEPARTED by David Bottrell and Jessie Jones

When Bud Turpin dies, his entire clan comes to the funeral. His son JUNIOR, in his twenties, is a dreamer, whose last project, running a machine that cleans parking lots, has been a huge bust. His wife Suzanne won't let him forget it. Here Junior talks to his brother Ray-Bud about an affair in which "one thing kinda led to another."

SCENE: In and around the towns of Lula and Timson, somewhere below the Mason-Dixon line. Ray-Bud's home.

TIME: The present. Night.

JUNIOR: Oh god. I don't know, Ray. It just sort of happened. I didn't plan it or anything. I was out in the K-Mart parking lot, giving them a free cleaning, sort of as a sample and she was loading some stuff into the back of her car. And she sort of struck up conversation. She asked my what I was doing. And I told her all about the machine and how it worked and she seemed real interested, you know. And Ray, I felt proud. Here I was sitting on top of this big piece of machinery and I was sort of the master of it, you know. And here was this woman looking up at me, smiling at me, making me feel like I was a man. A real man, like Daddy was. I was in business. I was a business man. I had control of my life.

[RAY-BUD: Well, what happened?]

Suzanne showed up! There she was looking all hot and wilted with all them kids hanging off her screaming for a Popsicle. And what did she want to talk about? The car payment. The house payment. Her mother. The kids needing this and needing that. And as she was talking, I watched this woman pack up the last of her stuff and just drive away. And all of a sudden I had this real strong desire to run Suzanne over with the machine.

[RAY-BUD: I can understand that, Junior.]

But see, it got worse. As the weeks went by, and things with the business started going sour, and the bills started piling up, all I could think about was killing Suzanne. Shooting her. Pushing her down the stairs. Sneaking up on her with a baseball bat. Just anything to shut her up.

[RAY-BUD: So what happened with the woman?]

One day, I just looked her up in the phone book. And one thing kinda led to another.

DEARLY DEPARTED by David Bottrell and Jessie Jones

When Bud Turpin dies, radio evangelist, REVEREND B.H. HOOKER delivers his eulogy. Here the Reverend does his radio show, including an advertisement for the funeral home.

SCENE: In and around the towns of Lula and Timson, somewhere below the Mason-Dixon line. A radio station.

TIME: The present. A quarter to midnight.

REVEREND: Real good, kids. Well, it's been a busy day and I've been in the car all day today, rushing from place to place, offering comfort and counsel to some of our brothers and sisters in crisis, catharsis and confusion.

As I sat in the various kitchens, offices and hospital rooms I was made aware of all the different kinds of problems we encounter here on this journey called life. And I said to myself, Beverly, what is this thing we call life. Is it nothing but a collection of problems, disappointments and heartache. Or do we make it that way with our endless wants, needs and desires. And if it is we ourselves who create all this unhappiness, why do we do it? Why don't we realize that the slender and fragile canoe of life can be so easily overturned in the turbulent rapids of the world. Why don't we just relax and take things as they come. And not expect so much. And why do we feel we have to call somebody when we're troubled? Why don't we just keep it to ourselves? Why do we feel the need to unload it on somebody and make them drive all the way out to our house on the hottest day of the year? Why do we cry and moan and bend somebody's ear till they think they're gonna die. Why don't we say to ourselves, before we pick up the phone, "Now is this really a problem or am I just bellyaching again?" Let us remember in these times of confusion, distress, and sorrow, that when it seems you can't go on, you probably can. And when you think to yourself, there's just no answer, you're probably right.

Remember friends, our time here is short. Shorter than any of us can imagine. And if you feel your life is nothing but a pit of unrelenting torture, try to make the most of it. After all, tomorrow is another day.

Alright. Now we got a lot more show for you, so don't go away. We're welcoming a new sponsor to the program tonight. (*reading from his notes*) Depew's Funeral Home. Where they combine a thrifty, no nonsense approach with Christlike sensitivity to answer your funereal needs. Alright, kids. Take us into the commercial.

DEATH AND THE MAIDEN by Ariel Dorfman

Paulina Escobar, around forty, was a victim of torture during the previous regime. Paulina recognizes the voice of her torturer when her husband brings home a stranger, DR. JORGE MIRANDA. Miranda stays for the night, during which Paulina ties him up. When he awakes, he's staring into the face of Paulina and a gun. To save his life, he must confess to being her torturer so he does. The question remains: is he telling the truth? Paulina's torturer would incessantly play "Death and the Maiden" while he "worked."

SCENE: A country that is probably Chile but could be any country that has given itself a democratic government just after a long period of dictatorship. A beach house by the sea.

TIME: The present.

(In the darkness, we hear Jorge's voice.)

JORGE'S VOICE: I would put on the music because it helped me in my role, the role of good guy, as they call it, I would put on Schubert because it was a way of gaining the prisoners' trust. But I also knew it was a way of alleviating their suffering. You've got to believe it was a way of alleviating the prisoners' suffering. Not only the music, but everything else I did. That's how they approached me, at first. The prisoners were dying on them, they told me, they needed someone to help care for them, someone they could trust. I've got a brother, who was a member of the secret services. You can pay the communists back for what they did to Dad, he told me one night—my father had a heart attack the day the peasants took over his land at Las Toltecas. The stroke paralyzed him—he lost his capacity for speech, would spend hours simply looking at me, and I was sure Dad was asking me when I would avenge him. But that's not why I accepted. The real real truth, it was for humanitarian reasons. We're at war, I thought, they want to kill me and my folk, they want to install a totalitarian dictatorship, but even so, they still have the right to some form of health care. It was slowly, almost without realizing how, that I became involved in more delicate operations, they let me sit in on sessions where my role was to determine if the prisoners could take that much torture, that much electric current. At first I told myself that it was a way of saving people's lives, and I did, because many times I told them—without it being true, simply to help the person who was being tortured—I ordered them to stop or the prisoner would die, but afterwards I began to—bit by bit, the virtue I was feeling turned into excitement—the mask of virtue fell off it and it, the excitement, it hid, it hid, it hid from me what I was doing, the swamp of what— . By the time Paulina Salas was brought in it was already too late. Too late.

(The lights go up as if the moon were coming out. It is nighttime. JORGE is in front of the cassette-recorder, still tied up, confessing.)

JORGE: ...too late. A sort of—brutalization took over my life, I began to really truly like what I was doing. It became a game. My curiosity was partly morbid, partly scientific. How much can this woman take? More than the other one? How's her sex? Does her sex dry up when you put the current through her? Can she have an orgasm under those circumstances? You can do what you want with her, she is entirely in your power, you can carry out all your fantasies... (*The moonlight begins to fade and only remains on the cassette-recorder, while Jorge's voice speaks on in the darkness.*) everything they have forbidden you since ever, whatever your mother ever urgently whispered you were never to do, you begin to dream with her at night, with all those women. Come on, Doctor, they would say to me, you're not going to refuse free meat, are you, one of them would sort of taunt me. His name was—let's see—they called him Bud, no, it was Stud— a nickname, because I never found out his real name. They like it, Doctor, Stud would say to me—all these bitches like it and if you put on that sweet little music of yours, they'll get even cozier. He would say this in front of the women, in front of Paulina Salas he would say it, and I finally, finally I—but not one ever died on me, not one...

(*The lights go up and it is now dawning. JORGE, untied, is writing on a piece of paper the words that come out of his voice from the cassette-recorder. In front of him, there is a pile of handwritten pages. PAULINA and GERARDO watch him.*)

JORGE'S VOICE (*from the recorder*): —not one of the women, not one of the men I was—looking after. As far as I can remember, I participated in the—interrogation of ninety-four prisoners, including Paulina Salas. It is all I can say. I ask forgiveness.

(*GERARDO switches off the cassette-recorder while Jorge writes.*)

DINOSAUR DREAMS by Tom Szentgyorgyi.

***

MARK, a lawyer in his twenties, lays out the harsh terrain and time in which this comedy occurs. He is speaking to his romantically troubled friend Bob.

SCENE: A bar after work. Background music: "Sledgehammer" by Peter Gabriel.

MARK: There's this guy in my office, older guy, been with the firm for years. He's your classic Wide Tie: house on the island, house upstate, kids at third-rate preps. Six figures of base, plus commissions, plus bonuses. Basically he's a porker, he's been a pig at the trough for the past ten years or so, and this has made him a very happy man. His grin is a decade wide.

But lately this guy has stopped grinning. Lately this guy has taken to wearing a face that I would call Permanently Creased. Anxiety lines have been ironed into it. The numbers are going bad, it's not so easy to be a wonder boy anymore, and word is the firm is going to drop his division. Just set it loose.

So the other day I'm in my office, I'm on the phone, talking the talk, when there's this…commotion. The hall is full of cops, paramedics, guys from maintenance, secretaries. The boys and girls are talking. He's jumped, he's got a gun, he's got a hostage. It's pandemonium. Turns out Wide Tie has barricaded himself in his office. He's shrieking about blood, investments, family, tax shelters he designed in 1972. He wants guarantees, he wants the governor and a supreme court justice on the floor in fifteen minutes.

It doesn't take long for this to get old. The special forces arrive. Guys in black and bulky Kevlar vests. They're very cool, very calm. Remarkably polite for men carrying automatic weapons. They have this device, it's like a huge rolling robot can opener, it pops the door, the guys go in. I cannot tell you how exciting this is. Wide Tie raises something and Johnny Swat, taking no chances, drops him then and there.

Turns out Wide Tie's weapon was a three-hole punch.

This causes some chagrin among the cop types. Suddenly everyone is very solicitous. They load Wide Tie onto a stretcher—there's blood everywhere—and roll him down the hall.

All the way down he keeps shouting, he will not shut up. "I'm sorry. I'm sorry. I'm sorry." Two weeks later his boys and girls are on the street. Couldn't be helped, the economy, the ecology, sunspots. Best of luck, fuck you all very much. Wide Tie, meanwhile, is resting comfortably at Our Lady of Perpetual Sedation. Which, considering the slate of civil and criminal suits he's facing, is probably the best place for him to be.

This man was unprepared for the days to come. This man looked in the mirror and failed to see what was looking back at him. Which was a thing incapable of adapting to a new environment. The colder world.

(*Beat.*)

I like his office. Door needs fixing, though.

THE END OF I by Diana Amsterdam

JEROME, in his late thirties, is in bed with his wife. He's going through a mid-life crisis.

TIME: The present.

JEROME: What is death? [ALICE: We'll figure it out in the morning.] You always say that. You always say we'll figure it out in the morning, but how will we figure it out? Do you know how to figure it out? I've been trying for three weeks to figure it out, and I can't figure anything out. I can't figure a damn thing out. Did it ever occur to you that death could be nothing? Nothing, Alice. Nothing. Nothing. Nothing. Death could be nothing. Nothing, Alice. Death could be absolutely nothing. Can you figure out nothing? Can you? Can you figure out nothing? Can you find nothing? Can you experience nothing? Can you *be* nothing? Try to *be* nothing. Go ahead, Alice. I dare you. Try it. (*ALICE is asleep.*) Try it. Try to be nothing. Try it. Just try it, Alice. Just try it. Just try it for one minute. For one second. Try it. Just try to *be* nothing. Not just nothing, nothingness. Try to be nothingness for one minute. For one second. Absolutely nothing. I don't mean something. I don't mean wake-up-in-a-few-hours. I mean nothing. Nothing. No thing, nothing. No feel. No smell. No taste. No see. No nothing. No nothing. No me. No I. No I. (*He bolts upright, extremely agitated.*) Alice. Alice. (*He shakes her awake.*)

[ALICE: Come here, darling.]

No! Don't tempt me! You fall into a woman's arms you can't even begin to understand nothing, nothing just disappears, nothing just evaporates, all around you there's something, something, something.

57

Women are very dangerous, Alice. (*ALICE is asleep.*) Women make you believe that you're going to live forever. And you're not going to live forever. You're going to die! Die! Die! Die! Die! Stay away from me, Alice! Alice. Alice! Oh God, I love you, I love you, Alice, I love you. I love you, I love you. I love you. I love you and I love our daughters. I love their eyes, I love their hair, I love their little fingernails. I love their tiny shoes. I love those little sheets you bought them, the ones with the butterflies. (*Notices the sheet under him.*) I love this sheet. I love this sheet! (*Rubs the sheet.*) I don't want to leave this sheet! I don't want to! I love it! I love this sheet! I don't want to! Would it go on without me? Could it go on without me? Could it? Would it? Where would I be? Where's Marty, Alice? What happened to Marty? Where did he go? One minute he was riding his motorcycle, zooming with the wind on his face more alive than at any other time except inside a woman and the next minute, blotto! Gone! Zap! Disappeared! *People disappear off this planet, Alice. All the time.* Can't you save me? Can't your love save me? Save me, Alice, save me! [ALICE: In the morning.] (*Speaks directly into her face.*) You and me are going to die, Alice.

THE EXTRA MAN by Richard Greenberg

JESS, in his twenties, wears his neuroses on his sleeve as he analyzes the dinner party Laura is giving in the next room. He's a critic for various arcane film magazines.

SCENE: The kitchen of Laura's apartment.

TIME: The present.

JESS (*enters*): Not that I don't love you, but your party makes me want to open a vein. Do you know what's going on out there? Okay. In the middle of the room, Paula Ellenbogen is holding forth on the topic of her recent dental surgery and displaying to anyone who'll take her up on it what she calls, "the gaping hole in my lower mandible." *Randy* is following Keith around the room, singing the overture to *Candide* or something into his ear—*directly* into his ear. And when

58

people look at Keith as if to suggest that this is, maybe, well, weird...disturbing... *painful*, he just looks back at them with this—is it forbearing or proud?—smile and continues whatever conversation he's engaged in as if nothing's happening. *Meanwhile* over by the pigs-in-the-blanket, appropriately enough, there is a pseudo-Marxist, dilettante, would-be documentary filmmaker who keeps pointing at me, no I swear it, and telling anyone who'll listen probably stuff like my latest piece in *FilmStream* is the tritest, most obvious, complacent piece of mainstream crap he's ever had the misfortune to read but don't bother to attack me for it, I'm too stupid to be attacked, I should just be pitied and laughed at. I mean, was this a campaign on your part to destroy my peace-of-mind? Do you hate me for some reason? Is this just the inevitable outcome of any gathering these days? Would you like to say something? Should I yield for an interjection?

FORTINBRAS by Lee Blessing

In this clever twist on *Hamlet*, FORTINBRAS, thirty, to whom Hamlet has bequeathed his kingdom, turns out to have flaws of his own. He refuses to believe Horatio's version of events—and to prove it, he declares war on Poland! Here he addresses the audience with his complaints while he copes with the ghost of Polonius invisible to everyone but him.

SCENE: King Fortinbras's chambers.

TIME: Shortly after Hamlet's death

FORTINBRAS: What am I going to do about Horatio? Why won't he *like* me?! Show a guy a little vision, and wham—he seizes up on you. He doesn't even want to talk to me now. Can't get his head out of the past. I hate the past, it's pointless, it's so...stiff. (*Looking around, to the audience.*) Something about this castle makes me want to talk to myself. Don't know why—I've spent my whole life *not* talking. Out on the battlefield, worried about spies behind every tentflap—all of them working for my uncle. I didn't dare say a word out loud. But here, the minute I'm alone I just...jabber. (*Suddenly calling out anxiously.*) Osric, where are my alternatives! (*To the audience again.*) I hope you don't think I'm callous, just because of those maidens. They really will have as good a time as can be expected. Under the circumstances. Given the point in history. I'm not known as Fortinbras the particularly Cruel or anything. I never used to do this sort of thing on my campaigns, but now that I'm King, it's sort of...expected. And it *has* been a long time. Honest. Not to get too personal. Anyway, I really will try to communicate with them. (*He hears shuffling in the hall.*) At last! (*POLONIUS appears.*) Not you again. (*POLONIUS stands attentively, smiles.*) Are you going to speak to me tonight? Are you ever going to speak to me? (*POLONIUS doesn't respond.*) What good is it if you won't tell me anything? (*POLONIUS shrugs, smiles, moves to the tapestry. He runs his hand over it.*) We keep going through this. What do you want? Do you have a dire warning? Is there a foul injustice? (*At "foul injustice" POLONIUS becomes exalted, as though he wants to speak.*) Yes? (*POLONIUS suddenly shrugs and waves it off with an "it's not that important" gesture.*) Damn it—! (*The two MAIDENS enter in nightdress looking anxiously at FORTINBRAS*) What do you want? Oh—sorry. In the bed. (*They follow FORTINBRAS's gesture and demurely jump into bed. Their wide eyes watch FORTINBRAS's every move. They do not see POLONIUS.*) I've got company now, you'll have to go. (*POLONIUS smiles, remains.*) I'm serious. The alternatives are here. (*No move by POLONIUS.*) You can't want to watch—you're dead!

FORTINBRAS by Lee Blessing

Fortinbras, to whom Hamlet has bequeathed his kingdom, has problems of his own. Not one ghost, as in Shakespeare's original, but twelve ghosts now constantly warn, exhort, admonish, and whine at Fortinbras. Here, POLONIUS complains about being dead. He examines the hole in the tapestry through which Hamlet stabbed him.

SCENE: A castle hall.

TIME: Shortly after Hamlet's slaying of Polonius.

POLONIUS: (*Touching it.*) Here. (*Touching his chest.*) Here. (*To the audience.*) It does something to a man's point of view when he suddenly feels a sword go through his heart. I was pinned like a bug against the wall. Where was all my good advice then? Stuck in my throat, where it's remained ever since. Oh, I still have plenty of advice, don't misunderstand. I could tell everybody in this castle, living and dead, what to do. But to hell with 'em, that's what I say. (*Sighing.*) If there were a hell. There doesn't seem to be, for me. No heaven either, that I've been able to discern. Only this—wandering around the scene of all my errors, watching everyone make the same old mistakes, *burning* to advise them—and hating myself for it. Death has been my greatest disappointment. It's too much like life. I thought there would be a great adventure, but there's no great adventure. I've asked the King, the Queen, the others—no one's had a great adventure. So far, there's been nothing to compare with that first moment, pinned against a wall, translated by a steel point—my face buried against the blank side of a tapestry—hoping that in a single instant all might finally be revealed. (*Tossing over the corner of the tapestry.*) What a hoax. Death has all the uncertainty of life, and twice the solitude. If you take my advice and no one ever does—you'll avoid it. (*POLONIUS turns to go.*)

A GENTILE OF THE TOP PERCENTILE by Bruce E. Whitacre

VAN BROOKS, a middle-aged former business executive, has abandoned the modern world and created an exact replica of the eighteenth century in his Fifth Avenue apartment: candlelight, servants, quill pens, period dress. Here, he explains his special refuge to his daughter:

TIME: The present.

VAN BROOKS: I inhabit that glorious moment of enlightenment, reason, Georgian enterprise, and grandeur, when poetry rhymed and kings ruled. I am an Augustan, dear child, out of time. Why, you ask? Why do I seek haven so in a world like this? Is it not apparent? Divorce? Losing thy mother and thee to Naporville? Illinois? What calamity. Oh, daughter, sheer calamity! And to hear thy bitter words enounced in a court of law! Against me! And to know the ensuing desolation was brought upon me in accordance with thine own will!

And those eyes—yea, my pretty, thine own in days of yore—had held all I had ever dreamt. Happily, I've now learnt one can dream new dreams, find new masks—But nay, twas not the donning of a mask. No, twas merely the exchanging of one for another. Man of enterprise, community, family, and electricity—Dynatech, you, your mother, all of it—became a man of single-minded eccentricity. Perfectly simple, enlightened: I exercise that right of freedom and choice the first Augustans devised, not so? "Pursuit of happiness." And indeed, I am truly happy to have thee here, just so...I'm...I do confess at first this antic pretention seemed but a temporary guise—one to doff and don as occasions arise. Yet over time it has become my solitary rod and staff, a prop, a ruse, aye, but all in all the best I had to choose. Now, thy comfort and aid do enliven me so that time without thee seems but a passage down a gloomy hall into this bright room. Welcome, my dear, obedient child. Time with thee is time beguiled. Now, as thy father, I must arrange for thee a suitable marriage.

GENTILE OF THE TOP PERCENTILE by Bruce E. Whitacre

RATHBONE, a twenty-five year old, very hot jazz musician, assures his upper crust girlfriend's father he can be trusted.

SCENE: Posh New York apartment.

TIME: The present.

RATHBONE: Yeah, me. Now listen. Just listen to me. Let me tell you what this is all about. I haven't had too good a life. Making a living in the arts...it's hell. But this morning, I saw something real. I saw this girl, this red dress girl, waiting for a cab. All I wanted was to lay on that red dress and feel it come off. Then I started talking to her. And, wow, she had things to say. She had this way of looking. She didn't know me, what I do, who I am, nothing. But she was so natural, so real. My mind—it just took off. We got in the cab and it was like our wedding day. I wanted to sit beside her all my life, through everything that's still to come: I'm talking marriage, twerps, right through mortgage in the burbs, man. Oh, shit, all that in one glance.

Unbelievable! But, no! So real. I forgot the fast life. She made me want to grow up, settle down, sink a few...roots. She changed my life, and all for the better. Babe—I mean, Reva, honey, come here. I think I love you, man, for real. (*They kiss.*) Now cut the blabber-talky and let's head out, okay?

THE GLORIOUS FOURTH by Robert Sugarman

JERRY, mid-thirties, a writer forced by the McCarthy blacklist to "ghost" for a living, reads a novel he hopes to adapt for the screen. He is trying to concentrate on the book, while at the same time making his daughter feel she has his undivided attention.

SCENE: East Hampton, Long Island. The beach.

TIME: 1957.

GERRY: I *didn't* watch honey, and the reason I didn't is that I have to read this. Today! I know what day it is, but I have to. I *was* watching, but I didn't see what you *just* did. ...you did it for the first time? If you do it again, you'll get my full attention. I promise. ...you will? Good. (*He sits up, leans forward*)

...*that was great.* I'd applaud, but this'll blow away. ... it's a new novel. ...it hasn't covers because it hasn't been published yet, these are *proof* sheets. ... no, it's *not* good, it's terrible. ...I'm reading it because I may be making a movie script from it, but it's a *secret*, so don't tell anybody. ...Scott, Jason, Kevin—any of your buddies, don't tell them. Promise? ...thanks. ...it's a secret because—because that's how things are these days.

...what you did? It was wonderful, what difference does it make what it's called. Names aren't everything. My name's not going to be on this script, but I'm going to write it. ...yes, I *would* like to have my name on it, I'd make more money and it's fun seeing my name up there on the screen. You're right, names *are* important, but I don't know what that's called. ...honey, if *you* don't know what it's called and you did it, how would a middle aged poop from Milwaukee know? You know so much stuff I don't. You grew up with pools and beaches,

63

I didn't. In Topeka we didn't *play* in water, we *washed* in it and we only did that when we could afford it. You know so much I never heard of. *Triceratops*. *Grand jete*. Do you think I had ballet lessons?

...damn right I suffered, that's why I'm resting. Well, I'm working, but I'm resting too. Watching, too. ...that's what grown ups do, lots of things at the same time. ...OK, I'll *only* watch and maybe the name'll come to me (*He folds the proofs around the notebook*) Take your time, deep breath, —GO!

...good, that's even better. ...no, the other wasn't bad, but you're experienced now, you present it better. You're a clever kid. Did I ever tell you that? ...can't help it, true is true, but if you arch your back more, it'll keep you straighter. Don't rush, take your time, deep breath—. ...that's it! I even know what it is. It's a *cartwheel*. We did those in Topeka in an empty lot filled with broken bottles. ...right, cut our hands all the time. All this sand—you got it so easy.

...excellent, straighter, but maybe that's enough for a while. People are designed to be upside down for limited periods of time. ...nobody told me, I just know. Isn't it great I'm here to share all this with you? I have to read now, OK? Believe me, I'd never read this if we didn't need the money. (*He resumes*)

...what? ...honey, I watched and I have to—. ...no, and I know this is a disappointment but your cartwheel is *not* sexy. It's athletic.

...if *what*? If you had *what*? ...honey, in public we call them (*softly*) "breasts." ...yeh, I guess then it would be sexy. ...who thought you were a boy? It's that dopey hair cut. "Gamin look"—you *are* a gamin. Old folks like Audrey Hepburn *need* to cut their hair like that, you don't.

...hot dogs? They're in the cooler, we'll cook them later. ...yes, I remembered the charcoal *and* the lighter stuff. ...you can't do cartwheels all that time, we're going to be here for hours. It has to be dark before they start the fireworks. Look at that sun—no!—*not directly*! It's going to be a long time. Can you see? I'm over here. Hi! Then comes the Big celebration—the Glorious Fourth. Did I tell you about the Glorious Fourth? ...I'm getting old, I forget. OK. One more.

...that was good. Sexy. It was....thank you, I will. (*He goes back to the proofs, realizes he must adjust the umbrella and gets up to do it*) ...this is *not* my only exercise. I swam—with you. Kids, no memory, no appreciation.

...Gwen, there is something I have to tell you. You've *always* been sexy. You were *born* sexy. ...you think I am? Thank you. Well, I used to be.

THE HOLY TERROR by Simon Gray

MARK MELON, in his forties, a publisher, has trouble organizing his talk to a women's group—a reflection of the trouble he has had in organizing his life. In fact, he is having a nervous breakdown.

SCENE: The Cheltenham Women's Arts Society. England.

TIME: The present.

MELON: Ms. Um, chairperson, ladies and—well, ladies, eh? First I am under instruction to tell you not to worry. When your delightful Mrs. Macdonald told me of the tradition of your teabreak, a tradition far more honored in the observing than in the breach, as Mrs. Macdonald wittily put it, I decided to play absolutely safe by bringing along this rather natty little alarm clock—a recent birthday present from someone—someone very dear to me—and I've set it to go off at four fifteen precisely. So don't be alarmed by the alarm, eh, it's rather loud and piercing, and rush for the exits thinking there's a fire or some such. Rush to the exits by all means, but only for your tea and sandwiches. There. We've got almost the most important thing out of the way haven't we? But I hope that the rest of what I say won't be just a way of filling time until the tea and sandwiches, oh, and cakes, too, I know, as Mrs. Macdonald allowed me a little peep at them on the way in, what a scrumptious selection—but even so, with those in prospect, I hope I'll be able to say something interesting about my life and times as a publisher. A little warning here, though, ladies. I'm not one for formal addresses, carefully structured and skillfully organized and meticulously rehearsed. All I've got to keep me on the straight and narrow, so to speak, are a few notes on a few cards, so that when I'm in danger of getting lost, or even worse, losing you, I can furnish myself with a little signpost and so point my nose back towards you, here in Chichester. Cheltenham, that is. So sorry, ladies. If I sometimes confuse them in my mind, it's only because they sound the same, and they share a tranquility, a charm, a peacefulness that is balm to the turbulent soul—so indeed I felt this morning, when I got off the train and treated myself to a little stroll along the leafy avenues. Such a relief from the broil and moil, the lunacy— (*KATE appears in the window right.*) um, chaos (*KATE disappears.*) of London life. As Kate, my wife Kate always used to say... (*KATE disappears from the window.*) Time for a card me thinks, eh? But where are they? I had them here. In my hand. I know I did. Ah yes. Here we are. Card number one. "Say sorry." Say sorry? But what for? I haven't said anything to say sorry for yet, have I? Oh, it must be to apologize in advance for some of the things I might suddenly find myself saying. Yes. Indeed. That's it—it must be. Because I've discovered from recent experience that one of the dangers of a free-wheeling style is that certain matters tend to bob up by association so to speak, that may be quite relevant—so I'm not talking about getting lost here—quite relevant, in fact of the utmost relevance but nevertheless be a trifle—a trifle unexpected. By being rather personal. So if I should find myself suddenly describing myself as behaving like a Hashemite widow, as I've been known to do when speaking publicly—known to describe myself, I mean, not actually *behave* like a Hashemite widow—good heavens, I hope not, no, no, that sort of thing is all very much in the past—I'm not actually sure, now that I've spoken the words, that I know what a Hashemite is, by the way. Do any of you ladies know what a Hashemite is? Oh, well, never mind. I'm sure we can all imagine how his widow would behave, can't we? Gosh, I feel comfortable! Here in this room with so many kind and interested ladies—at least you look interested, thank you for that—there was a time, you know, and not so long ago either, when I would have laughed out loud at the thought of standing here in front of you today. Yes, I would not only have thrown an invitation to address the Chichester—Cheltenham Women's Institute straight into the wastepaper basket, but I'd have made a bawdy joke or two into the bargain. You can guess the sort of thing. Well, I can tell you ladies, not any more. Things have changed. It's not my habit these days to make jokes about women, or indeed about sex. There seems to me nothing funny to be found in either, so never fear, ladies, you won't be getting any bawdiness from me! But now you're probably saying to yourself, "Oh, I do wish the silly fellow would stop telling us what he's not going to tell us, and just get on with it and tell us what he is going to tell us." And if you're not it's only because you're too kind and patient. So why don't I just leap in and—and—now where did I intend to start? Oh yes. Conquering all before me. Perhaps I shouldn't have read that out, it does sound so immodest, doesn't it—But the truth is, it's the truth.

I HATE HAMLET by Paul Rudnick

A huge New York apartment is haunted by the ghost of John Barrymore. Its new tenant, ANDREW RALLY, a TV star in his late twenties, is persuaded by Barrymore to play Hamlet in Central Park. After the first performance, Gary analyzes his performance.

TIME: The present.

ANDREW: Last night, right from the start, I knew I was bombing. I sounded big and phony, real thee and thou, and then I started rushing it, hi, what's new in Denmark? I just could not connect. I couldn't get ahold of it. And while I'm...babbling, I look out, and there's this guy in the second row, a kid, like 16, obviously dragged there. And he's yawning and he's jiggling his legs and reading his program, and I just wanted to say, hey kid, I'm with you, I can't stand this either! But I couldn't do that, so I just keep feeling worse and worse, just drowning. And I thought, okay, all my questions are answered—I'm not Hamlet, I'm no actor, what am I doing here? And then I get to the soliloquy, the big job, I'm right in the headlights, and I just thought, oh Christ, the hell with it, just do it!

    To be or not to be, that is the question;
    Whether 'tis nobler in the mind to suffer
    The slings and arrows of outrageous fortune,
    Or to take arms against a sea of troubles
    and by opposing, end them.

And I kept going, I finished the speech, and I look out, and there's the kid—and he's listening. The whole audience—complete silence, total focus. And I was Hamlet. And it lasted about ten more seconds, and then I was back in Hell. And I stayed there. But for that one little bit, for that one speech—I got it. I had it. *Hamlet.* And only eight thousand lines left to go. (*The preceding monologue must grow extremely passionate; ANDREW must be transported back to the previous evening onstage.*)

THE INNOCENTS CRUSADE by Keith Reddin

BILL at sixteen is making the rounds with his parents of college admissions offices. Here, he is selling himself to an admissions officer.

SCENE: An Ivy League campus.

TIME: The present.

BILL: You see I have all this talent. I can sit down in front of a piano and look at the music and play it, play it very well. I started lessons very young because my parents saw I had this natural ability. I had an affinity with music. And I suppose I could have pursued a career, very successfully, as a concert pianist if I wanted to, but I realized that I would have to give everything up, everything but my music, and I wasn't prepared for that, you know? Also, I can draw very well. You give me a sketch pad and a piece of charcoal and I could do a remarkable likeness of you. I am physically very active. I tried out for several different teams at the school, I like tennis, I play a wicked tennis game, I'm a real net man, I have this killer instinct, and that gets me into trouble in a doubles game, but what can you do? I was on the school paper, I was one of the editors, and I wrote articles, articles on politics, that's something I might go into down the line because I have this talent for public speaking, for conveying ideas, and journalism, I could be a journalist, because I write well, I have the knack to form ideas and communicate them in terse, concise language that has been called forceful. And languages. I'm a natural with languages. I studied several, but I was thinking of concentrating on Latin, I think Latin is very underrated right now, I think it's due for a comeback, don't you? I mean, I think these things go in cycles, for awhile Spanish and Chinese were all the rage, but I think it's time for the pendulum to swing back to the basics, to Latin. I was thinking about becoming a classical scholar, something like that. Then there's the sciences, I'm pretty exceptional with abstract concepts, physics, particle physics, could do that or maybe nuclear physics, that's important or astrophysics. Did you read that book *A Brief History of Time*, by Stephen Hawking? Neither did I, I couldn't get past page fifteen, I haven't met anybody who could finish it, it was incomprehensible to me, yes, the man is brilliant I'm sure, but that book, it was a best seller but I don't think anybody really read it, do you? Then there's history and chemistry and cartography and medicine, I could go into that, I could have a very rewarding career in any of those fields, but here's my problem. What do I focus on? Granted, I could be one of those all around multi-career type people, but in order to be the best in the field, I think I should narrow my energies to one field of study. But which one, that's the question. Because if I choose one over another, am I then depriving myself and in a way, the world, am I depriving all of us of some insight, some discovery, some creation, something that would lie, you know, dormant till I came along? This is the dilemma I face.

JOINED AT THE HEAD by Catherine Butterfield

JIM, in his thirties, overhears his wife, Maggy, telling a high school friend how well she is faring in her battle with cancer. Jim now relates his own version of Maggy's progress.

SCENE: Their Boston apartment.

TIME: The present.

JIM: Here's what you won't hear from them about me. You won't hear about the nights I lie awake looking at Maggy, thinking about what a wonderful mother she would have made. Or how beautiful our children would have been. You won't hear about how I lust for her, even now, even with tubes running out of her body. How I fantasize

69

about making her well with my ejaculations, as though it were a life-giving fluid that could wash through her entire body and render her clean again. Or about the other side of that, the self-hatred that goes along with forcing yourself upon a sick person. Even though she pretends it's voluntary, that she wants it, too. You won't hear about the anger, an anger so strong and vicious it feels like it could wipe out cities. Anger at the world, at fate, at this fucking roll of the dice that is your life. And anger at Maggy, for letting herself get so sick. For doing this to me and ruining my life. You particularly won't hear about this last because I don't tell it to anyone, least of all myself. You won't hear about my dreams, dreams of flight, of other women, of another life, the one with her we didn't get to have. You won't know what comfort I take in these dreams, the true happiness I find in them. And the strange sensation of waking up to discover that it's your life that is the nightmare, not the dream. "Don't cry, Jim, it's only your life. You're asleep now, everything's okay." You won't hear about the people I work with, and how they've reacted to all this. How some are compassionate and caring, and others treat me like I'm perhaps a carrier and they're going to get it themselves. Still others act as though nothing has happened, and I'm probably overreacting. And more than one woman is already shooting up flares—"I'm available when all this is over!" Vulture women. If they knew my fantasies regarding them, every sphincter would open in abject fear. You won't hear about the effort it takes to stay positive, to keep hoping, to never let her know I've given up. And you won't know, because she couldn't possibly realize herself, how desperately and deeply I love her. My partner. My life partner. The one I'm joined to forever. My love. My wife. (*He takes another drink from the water fountain, slicks back his hair*) I just thought you should know.

LA BÊTE by David Hirson

VALERE, a vain, talkative, and absolutely indomitable traveling actor is vehemently criticized by Elomire, a fellow actor. VALERE asks Elomire to kindly write down his comments. Elomire asks, whatever for.

SCENE: France. Outside the actors' dining room.

TIME: 1654.

Author's Note: "This play is meant to be performed in an absurdly high comic style, at lightning speed and with rhymes and iambs stressed. The costumes are 17th-century bouffe—powdered wigs, etc. The pace is frantic."

VALERE: Because I'm anxious to *improve*!
Is that so strange, my wanting to remove
The flaws from my persona? Surely not!
I loathe a blemish! I despise a spot!
Perfection is the goal towards which I strive
(For me, that's what it means to be alive)
And, hence, I'm grateful for a shrewd critique:
It keeps my talent honest, so to speak!
We of the theatre share that common view—
The criticisms of the things we do
Inspire our interest, not our hurt or rage:
We know it's part of "being on the stage"
To have oneself assessed at every turn,
And thus we show a willingness to learn
From judgments which might wound another man.
I much prefer to any drooling fan
A critic who will SLICE me into parts!
GOD *LOVE* THE CRITICS! *BLESS* THEIR PICKY HEARTS!
Precisely, and in no uncertain terms,
They halve the apple, showing us our worms.
(*Staggering slightly*)
(My God, that was a *brilliant* illustration!)
(*Regaining himself.*)
Don't get me wrong: to hear some dissertation
On all one's failings gives a twinge of course:
It smarts when someone knocks you off your horse—
That's true for anybody I should think!
But climbing on again in half a wink
And knowing that you're better for the spill

Instructs us that it's love and not ill-will
That motivates a critical assault.
You've *honored* me tonight by finding fault!
Which doesn't mean I don't feel vaguely crushed...
I *do!* I'm *bruised!* But who would not have blushed
To hear himself discussed so centrally?
"My God," I thought, "Are they denouncing *me*,
These men of such *distinction* and *renown*!?
How thrilling I'm the one they're tearing down!!
What joy that Elomire, whom people say
Is destined to become the next Corneille,
Should slander *me* in such a public forum!"
And, by the way, it isn't just decorum
Which prompts me to express my awe of you;
Your plays, I think, show genius, and a few
(Like *Mandarin*) I've seen five times or more.
Now there's a play that really made me roar!
I haven't laughed so hard in years and years!
[Elomire: It was a tragedy.]
                              But through my *tears*
The laughter seemed more painful... (O MY GOD!
WELL, OPEN MOUTH, INSERT THY FOOT, YOU CLOD!
COULD THAT HAVE BEEN MORE AWKWARD? SURELY NOT!
(*Fanning himself*)
I'M *SO* EMBARRASSED! WHEW! MY FACE IS HOT!)
Forgive me, Elomire. What can I say?
I'm sure it was a very solemn play.
But why, then, did I find it such a hoot?
The crippled peasant boy who played the flute:
Hysterical! I mean I was delirious!
I must have nodded off when it got serious!
Are you quite sure it was a tragedy?

LAST CALL FOREVER by Leonard Melfi

Five smalltown young people encounter each other for the first time and

face the same problem—the death of a loved one. Their youth has left them unprepared for their loss.

CHUBBY CHARLESTON, a nice-looking nighttime bartender in his late twenties, is about to go home alone at two after giving "last call" for alcohol.

SCENE: A bar in upstate New York.

TIME: The present. Two-something in the morning

CHUBBY: (*A pause.*) Well, after my mother's funeral I didn't know what I was going to do. At first I thought that it didn't happen. Then I thought—because I realized that it did happen!—that I would go out of my mind before the day was over with. Once I got that idea out of my mind, well...it got worse, if you can believe it!...things got worse: I decided I wanted to commit suicide. I was going to drink and drink and drink, and then I was going to kill myself. (*A pause.*) But...and here we go now!...I think—I know!—that my guardian angel came to my rescue. Oh, God: I really believe in everybody's own personal guardian angel! Mio Guardian Angelo! What a pure blessing! I could almost hear him whisper in my ear, both ears, in fact. He kept running from my left side to my right side in order to make sure that I got his message. He told me to get on a Greyhound bus that night. He told me to pack an overnight bag and to take the bus down to the Big Apple for a sudden change of scenery and everything else. He whispered to me that it would really do me good, that it would be the best thing for me...and I believed him, too!...I took his word for it. He was like a whisper of vermouth in the perfect gin martini. He was just plain fabulous: my special, private, own personal guardian angel! (*A pause.*) And so, I bought my round-trip ticket—and it was just getting nice and dark outside now—and with my little overnight bag, and, of course, with my guardian angel, I got on the bus. I decided to sit in the back. It was empty—those three seats side-by-side—and so, I figured I'd have the whole area to myself, all the way down to the Big Apple. A few minutes went by when I saw this pretty nice-looking girl heading towards the back of the bus. She was dark-haired and it was in a pony-tail and she looked like a student in her early twenties

73

somewhere. She also had a little overnight bag, sort of like mine. She looked down at me, and then she said: "Is anybody sitting there?" and, naturally, she meant the empty seat next to me, even though there were other empty seats on the bus, and some of them even next to the window. And do you know something? I knew right then and there what she had on her mind! I let her know that the seat next to me was not taken. She placed her little overnight bag on the shelf above our seats, and then she sat down next to me, to my right, while I tried glancing in my reflection in the window of the bus to my left, hoping that I looked pretty good for her. I even wet my lips a couple of times to see how they look in the window reflection, and which also helped me get in the mood that I wanted to get into. She didn't have to worry. She was in that certain mood from the very beginning. Ah! What a trip! The girl in her very early twenties, and me: pushing forty. I always dreamed of something like this. Before we got to Scranton, she pretended she was sleeping, and she dropped her head on my shoulder. I started to get a hard-on—I'm sorry, I mean an erection!—and then before I knew it I found my lips on her face, and then before I knew it again, we were both kissing each other on the lips like two crazy nuts, breathing real heavy, and then she came up for air, and she whispered to me: "No one will ever know," and then she unzipped my fly, and I pulled down her panties, and she moved over, and she sat on top of my erection—I mean hard-on!—and we lasted that way all through Pennsylvania, and the Delaware Water Gap, and the Poconos, and Strousbourg, and New Jersey...oh, my God!...all the way through the inside of the Lincoln Tunnel, which just happened to be the best part of it all! And that's it, everybody!

LIFE DURING WARTIME by Keith Reddin.

Gale, a single mother, is pestered and prodded by her son HOWARD, sixteen, to inquire about his day. Gale asks. Here's Howard's answer.

SCENE: Gale's living room.

TIME: The present.

HOWARD: Okay. Barry and me after school, we're driving around. We're driving on the Parkway and we're in the left lane and Barry's going fast, maybe a little too fast. I say Barry slow down, but he's trying to pass this car in the passing lane and it doesn't move over so Barry puts on his lights, he's flashing his lights at this guy to pull over so we can pass and I go Barry, take it easy, but now like Barry is pissed, and we are tooling along and this other car it pulls alongside us and there's some guys in there and they are very pissed off so we take off dueling back and forth like who can get in front of the other and Barry he goes mental and tries to push this car onto the shoulder and then he sort of bumps the car, well he crashes into the side of it, and we both pull over and Barry is incensed but I tell Barry I want to just get the fuck out of here and we get out and the guys from the other car get out only there's four of them and two of us, and this one guy the driver goes up to Barry and puts his face close up to Barry's face and says you fucked with the wrong person today and these guys push Harry and me up against their car and then from out of their trunk they take this wire and they tie our hands behind our backs and they hit Barry in the head and they put us in the trunk and say we're going for a ride fuckface and they drive us for about half an hour and then I hear this gravel crunching and we stopped and they open the trunk and these four guys push out into these woods and Barry's pissing in his pants and I'm thinking we're dead you know, so this guy with funny teeth he pulls out a gun and he puts it to Barry's head and tells him hey pussy you scraped the side of our car what are you going to do about it and Barry and me we don't say nothing and these other guys say if we don't want to die we have to eat dirt and so we do, we eat dirt and these other guys get real quiet and watch us eat dirt and then they piss on Barry and they push this gun in Barry's face and then they smoke some cigarettes and don't talk then they get in their car and drive off. And after a while we get up and start walking down the road and look for a cop car but we couldn't find one so we start hitching and we get a ride and we walk a ways to Barry's car with this huge damage done to its side and he drives back to here and tells me not to say anything about this ever, but it's just too incredible you know, so I'll be in my room till dinner.

LIFE DURING WARTIME by Keith Reddin:

A young salesman, Tommy, commits a burglary, which inadvertently leads to the death of his girlfriend and her son. The outpouring of his guilt is periodically interrupted by JOHN CALVIN, the sixteenth-century religious philosopher, in his forties, who makes the following observations:

SCENE: A lecture hall.

TIME: The present.

CALVIN: When Adam fell he did not merely succumb to a lower appetite but unspeakable impiety occupied the very citadel of his mind and pride penetrated to the depths of his heart. Although I do not think that man is without goodness, I do think that no human activity is blameless. We have reason, but reason is overwhelmed by so many deceptions, subjected to so many errors, dashed against so many obstacles, caught in so many difficulties it can no longer guide us. It is our destiny to sin. Also I find the increasingly graphic representation of violence in motion pictures and television disturbing. Films like *To Live and Die in L.A.*, or a series such as *Miami Vice* seem to, in some unconscious way, condone violence against mankind. Younger viewers like Howard constantly watching this sort of thing become numbed by these acts of brutality and so picking up a gun and shooting someone's face off means nothing. I also thought *Year of the Dragon* was too violent. Although I was impressed by the technical quality of the film, and I admired Micky Rourke's performance. The use of profanity in this film corrupts language and deadens our senses. But as I've said due to original sin we have no free will to better ourselves, so there you are. Our mind even when it comprehends the enormity of sin, cannot move the will to reject it. Sinfulness means the proclivity to sin, and the potential for sinfulness. Every human being at every moment is on the verge of sinning. Still, do we really need a film like *Texas Chainsaw Massacre Part II*? Think about it.

John Calvin on Drama. The idea of play and playing troubles me. The stage encourages the sinful practices by which human beings pretend to be that which they are not in order to deceive and exploit. It is false and dangerous to create fantasies, inventions, that cause audiences to weep or laugh. Poets invent whatever suits them and thus have filled the world with the grossest and foulest errors. I hate hypocrisy. Hypocrisy is the essence of one who plays at something he is not. He trivializes existence, which is not as some of them would have you believe a farce, or "only a game." The antidote to this hypocrisy is self-examination. Only by being ruthlessly honest with ourselves instead of playing at something or someone else can we begin to find God. I wish I could say things are going to get better, that you might be comforted, but that would be a falsehood. Things are only going to get worse. Much worse. Now that's the truth.

LIPS TOGETHER TEETH APART by Terrence McNally

SAM TRUMAN, his wife Sally, his sister Chloe, and Chloe's husband John—all in their late thirties—are spending the July 4th weekend at the Long Island beach house which belonged to Sally's brother, who died of AIDS.

On the deck of the beach house, Sam, a self-employed businessman, in a soliloquy the others cannot hear, speaks to his pregnant wife Sally, who he knows is having an affair with John.

TIME: The present.

SAM: My brain has become a collision course of random thoughts. Some trivial, but some well worth the wonder. Sometimes I think I'm losing my mind. I'm not sure of anything anymore. It's the same anxiety I have when I think I've forgotten how to tie my tie or tie my shoelaces or I've forgotten how to swallow my food and I'm going to choke on it. Three days ago I was standing in front of our bathroom mirror in terror because I couldn't knot my tie. I wanted to say "Sally, please come in here and help me." But I couldn't. What would she have thought? Last night I spit a piece of steak into my napkin rather than risk swallowing it, because I was afraid I would choke. Maybe it's trivial and that's why no one wants to talk about it, so I'm talking to myself. No one wants to listen to who we really are. Know somebody really. Know you leave shit stains in your underwear and pick your nose. Tell a woman you've forgotten how to swallow your food and she's in her car and out of your life before you can say "Wait, there's more. Sometimes I have to think about someone else when I'm with you because I'm afraid I won't stay hard if I don't. Or how much I want to fuck the teenage daughter of the couple that lives three doors down. How my father takes all the air out of the room and I can't breathe when I'm with him. How if I could tear my breast open and rip out my heart and feed it to these sea gulls in little raw pieces, that pain would be nothing to the one I already feel, the pain of your betrayal! How most afraid I am of losing you." How can I tell you these things and there be love?

THE LITTLE TOMMY PARKER CELEBRATED COLORED MINSTREL SHOW by Carlyle Brown

HENRY, a minstrel performer in his sixties, is shining his shoes and popping a rag to the beat of a banjo, played by another minstrel man.

SCENE: The interior of an open-ended replica private Pullman car of the late nineteenth century. This is the traveling home of the black minstrel performers.

TIME: 1895.

HENRY: That song put me to mind when I was a kid shining shoes outside the 11th Street Opera House in Philadelphia. I wasn't no older than that boy Archie. There was some big-time minstrel group playin' in the Opera House and the place was slowly gettin' packed. I was makin' as much as a nickel a shine. There was this old colored man standing just a little ways from where I had my shine box set up. And he was just a shoutin', "Place ya bets. Place ya bets. Boy can play the coronet while jiggin'. With every note and every beat as clear as if each had been done alone. Not a slur or stumble will you hear, but only the sweet soundin' noise of the most educated music. Place ya bets. Place ya bets." Well, he was a funny lookin' old colored man and

78

he was standin' right next to the playbill of the Opera House where they had a picture of the minstrel group blacked up and another one of them in they regular face. Everybody had to pass me and him to get into the theatre. He was attracting a whole lot of attention, funny lookin' the way he was, standin' next to that playbill and shoutin'. "Place ya bets, place ya bets." Pretty soon he had him a crowd and I was shinin' a lot a shoes.

Before ya know it, some of these high class gentlemen is makin' jokes 'bout this old colored man. "You can't play and dance." You can't do this and you can't do that. But they was holdin' up their money to bet. When time come for that old colored man to cover them bets, he walk over to me and he say, "Boy, what's yo name?" I say, "Henry." He say, "I'm glad to know you, Henry. My name is Moe. Moe Joe Jefferson. Moses Joseph Jefferson. It's a good Christian-American name," he say. He say, "I know you hear me braggin', but I can play this horn and do a jig for truth. And I can win me that money, 'cause they don't believe in me, but I do."

He say, "All I need from you is ya shine money to cover them bets." I said, "My shine money, you can't take away my shine money." He say, "I'll double ya shine money, boy. Besides, you wasn't shinin' no shoes at all, till I come along with this here crowd." He say, "Don't holler 'bout what's fair, just be fair." It was a strange way a lookin' at things, but I know'd somehow he was right and I give him my shine money. He played a tune something like the one you strummin', Tambo. And his jig sound just like a man playin' the trap drum. Here's my hand to God, it sound just like a wailin' trap drum. He wasn't just playin' and dancin' at the same time. He was havin' a duet with hisself. A duet between his mouth and his feet. One time he took that horn out his mouth and he say, "Shine ya shoes, Henry, shine ya shoes. Make ya self some shine money." Well folks watching that old colored man puts they feet on my shine box and I shine and I pop my rag to the beat and now me and Moe Jefferson is a trio. Folks forgot all about the minstrel show, they was havin' a ball with me and Moe Joe. That old colored man dance his natural behind off. He cut the most amazing steps you ever saw. Played and did flips and never missed a note. And his music. His music was different. He put his stressin' in a lot a funny places, so it had a raggedy, loose kinda sound, like a stumblin', strong, drunk man refusin' to fall. Like that music they call rag, that they play in the houses and the parlors. Man, the people was all off the sidewalk and out all into the street. Inside, the Opera House was almost empty. The theatre manager come with the police and make us get from round there. But hell, it didn't do em no good, 'cause the crowd come with us. We was out in the streets, so Negroes was allowed to see our show. In fact, it was the most mixed house I ever saw. All wanted to see Moe Joe Jefferson do his thing. We fell into this saloon down 11th Street and once that owner saw that crowd, he didn't mind no colored in his place that night. There was this other old colored man in there, hunched up at the piano. One of his legs was way shorter than the other and he didn't have but three fingers on his left hand. He caught on quick to what was goin' on, and boy, we was now a regular goddamn band.

Moe Jefferson danced on top a the tables, on the bar. Seem like he was dangling off the ceiling and around the walls, too. I popped my little dere rag, 'til I couldn't pop no more. My arms was like lead. I musta fell asleep in all that ruckus. I woke up in a corner with Moe Joe's coat coverin' me. The place was empty 'cept for the porter. Everybody was gone. The crowd, Moe Joe Jefferson, and my shine money.

THE LOMAN FAMILY PICNIC by Donald Margulies

HERBIE, the man of the house, is an appliance fixtures salesman. His wife Doris is a depressive who fantasizes about leaving him, but that's okay since he fantasizes about leaving her too. His son Mitchell is writing a musical version of *Death of a Salesman*, called *Willy!*, and his other son, Stewie, is about to have a Bar Mitzvah Herbie can't afford.

Here, Herbie, as he is dressing to go to work, stops, holding one sock, lost in thought.

SCENE: A highrise apartment in Coney Island.

TIME: Around 1965.

HERBIE: (*To us.*) Maybe I don't have dreams anymore. I mean I must, but I don't remember. I don't remember a thing. My childhood? The war? Show me a picture of me taken someplace and I couldn't tell you where. I won't remember the name of the buddy I had my arm around. Ask me what year my kids were born, I couldn't tell you. Either of them. I know I was married eighteen years ago 'cause that's what Doris told me; the other night was our anniversary. I know how old I am; I'm forty years old. I was born in '25, but the exact date they're not sure, and the midwife who signed the birth certificate put my sex down as female. So I don't know; I don't know. I remember Dame May Whitty was in *The Lady Vanishes*...but I don't remember my father even shaking my hand. [STEWIE: (*To Mitchell.*) He's crazy. Let's face it. He's gone. Lost in action] (*To us.*) Did *my* father throw *me* a bar mitzvah? I don't even remember *being* bar mitzvahed. If I *was* you can be sure nobody thought twice about it. They say we were very poor when I was young. (*Shrugs.*) I don't remember. Supposedly we were on relief. Six kids in three rooms. No doors. No privacy. Hand-me-downs from my brothers...Nothing ever started with me, it ended with me. I didn't have much; that much I remember. You stop *wanting,* so what you don't *have* doesn't matter. This is the Depression I'm talking about. I got through those years with my eyes shut tight and holding my breath like when you're under water. Got the hell outta *there*, straight to the Army. War was an improvement. Then I met Doris, then I married her, got this job, kids...And I go through every day with my eyes shut tight and holding my breath, till the day is over and I can come home. To what? What kind of home is left to come home to by the time I come home?

LOST IN YONKERS by Neil Simon

Grandma Kurnitz, a German-Jewish tyrant, has taken in her son Eddie's two boys, while he goes away. Another son, LOUIE, in his thirties, is a bag man for the mob. He has come home to escape being killed by gangsters. He meets his nephews for the first time in years.

SCENE: A house in Yonkers, New York, that sits above Kurnitz's Kandy store.

TIME: 1942.

LOUIE: I never said she was a lot of laughs. I'll tell you the truth. I don't like her much myself. She knows it. Why should I? She used to lock me in a closet for breakin' a dish. A ten-cent dish, I'd get two, three hours in the closet. And if I cried, I'd get another hour... No light, no water, just enough air to breathe. That's when I learned not to cry. And after a few times in the closet, I toughened up. But I also never broke another dish... No, I didn't like her, but I respected her. Hell of a teacher, Ma was. [ARTY: Wouldn't it have been easier if she bought paper plates?] Then where's the lesson? There's no respect for paper plates. Hear me out... She was no harder on us than she was on herself. When she was twelve years old, her old man takes her to a political rally in Berlin. The cops broke it up. With sticks, on horseback. Someone throws a rock, a cop bashes in her old man's head, a horse goes down and crushes Ma's foot. Nobody ever fixed it. It hurts every day of her life but I never once seen her take even an aspirin...She coulda had an operation but she used the money she saved to get to this country with her husband and six kids. That's moxie, kid.

THE MAN WHO COULDN'T DANCE by Jason Katims

ERIC and Gail, in their thirties, former lovers, stand over the crib of Gail's baby, Elizabeth, whom she has had with her new husband, Fred. Eric starts to cry after picking Elizabeth up. After replacing the baby in the crib, he tries to explain his reaction.

SCENE: The converted attic of Gail's house in Connecticut.

TIME: The present.

ERIC: I can't dance, Gail. [GAIL: You can't dance. This is why you're crying? Eric, a lot of people can't dance.] I don't know why I can't dance. But it's—I can't. I can't make my body move in these ways that the music is demanding that I move. It's just so goddamn embarrassing. The situation. I mean, standing in public around hundreds of people who are displaying their purest, truest selves. I mean, it takes them no more than two drinks and their souls are out there on the dance floor. Their goodness. Their sensuality. They're sharing and loving. I watch that, look at that. But my body fights it. I start to analyze the music. The rhythm. The time signature. I understand the theory of dancing. The *idea* of spontaneously sharing in this moment that exists now and only now. The give and take with your partner. Two mirrors on a land where gravity holds you to this point and then leaves you free. And that the universe happens right there and then. Like, truth. I understand this intellectually. But Gail, I never have experienced it. I can't dance. [GAIL: How did Elizabeth make you think of that?] When we were together. There were all these times when you would arrange for us to be in these places. These parties. And invariably there would be a band, or music playing and invariably people would start dancing. [GAIL: I would arrange this? Like I did this to you?] Invariably you would want to dance. And I wouldn't dance with you. I wouldn't dance with you, Gail. And I could see the hurt register on your face. I could see the anger build within you. I could see that this just wouldn't do for you. [GAIL: Why didn't you just say I can't dance. Why didn't you just tell me?] Because it was the dam holding the water. If I let that out. That one thing, everything would follow. I couldn't dance. I couldn't have a normal talk about the weather with a neighbor without getting into a conversation about God, love, and eternity. I mean, after all, the weather has these huge connotations. I couldn't act correctly in social situations. I couldn't sacrifice truth for a relationship. I couldn't hold you when you needed to be held because I wanted you to be stronger. Because I wanted to be stronger. I couldn't ask you for the warmth of your touch out of need. I couldn't let myself. I would only ask for your touch out of strength. Out of something that wouldn't become sick and interdependent and symbiotic. I wasn't able to do these things. I don't know, Gail. I mean, you marrying Fred didn't really say anything to me. It was like something in this continuum. This cycle. I mean, it was this thing that happened in my life. The love of my life got married to another man. It didn't seem permanent. But the fact that Elizabeth…The fact that this angel…this unbelievable gift isn't mine. And will never be mine. This is killing me. [GAIL. Oh my God, Eric. You're human.] I'll never have a daughter, Gail. [GAIL: Yes, you

83

will.] I'm thirty-seven. I have done nothing but make myself more isolated, unavailable, and unappealing. Believe it or not, it's difficult picking up women with this type of conversation. I work for four dollars an hour, Gail. I never earned a college degree. I can't bring myself to work for someone who is not producing something with some kind of goodness. That rules out ninety-eight percent of job openings. And the other two percent pay approximately four dollars an hour. I am not really going to change. I don't know why this is. People think I make these choices. But you've got to believe me, Gail, I have no control. I can't dance.

MARVIN'S ROOM by Scott McPherson

Bessie takes care of her father, Marvin, after his stroke. When Bessie develops leukemia, her sister Lee and Lee's son, HANK, come to Florida to see if they can provide bone marrow to save her. Hank, a disturbed boy of seventeen, who burned down his family's house has come from a mental institution.

Here, before the bone marrow test, HANK tells Bessie about life in the institution.

SCENE: Doctor's waiting room.

TIME: The present.

HANK: Bugs don't bother me. [BESSIE: No?] They crawl out of the drain in the boys' shower. They hide in the lumber in the wood shop. They float in the soap basins on the sinks. You get used to them. [BESSIE: I wouldn't.] One dude in my room—there's twelve of us in this room, and this one dude catches bugs and puts them on a leash. [BESSIE: A leash?] A hair leash. He pulls out a strand of his hair and ties it around the bug and the other end he tacks down under his bunk. He had this whole zoo of bugs walking in little circles under his bed. [BESSIE: Hank.] Till this other dude smashed them all with the back of this cafeteria tray. It was funny. [BESSIE: Sounds funny.] It's not like anybody ate off the tray. It was an old tray. We use it to slide

84

down the mud hill behind the seizure ward. [BESSIE: Uh-huh.] You get going real fast. This one dude's old man used to clock pitches for the National League East. He clocked me with his radar gun going fifty. [BESSIE: That's fast.] And my tray shot out from underneath me and broke this dude's windpipe. We had to perform an emergency tracheotomy with a sharp piece of bark and a Bic pen. [BESSIE: Hmmm.] Man, it was something. You want a candy? (*He offers her a candy from the nursing home*)

MY SIDE OF THE STORY by Bryan Goluboff

AARON ACKERMAN, 25, a stockbroker in his father's business, tries to cheer him up after the older man has seen Aaron's mother, his wife, with another man. They share reminiscences and Aaron describes how he first knew that his romance with his own true love, Emily, was over.

SCENE: The bathroom of his father's apartment.

TIME: The present.

AARON: Shit… Alright, well, basically, when I met her she had a lotta problems, she thought she was stupid, fat and ugly. So for two and a half years I told her she was brilliant, thin and beautiful, which was the truth. When I finally convinced her, she didn't need me around anymore. I remember the exact date—February 20, 1990. 'Cause that's the night Mike Tyson lost his title. I went over to her place—She said she had "Something to talk to me about." Never good news, you know? She didn't waste time, she brought the whip right down— "Freedom," "Curiosities about other men," the usual buzzwords. "Friends"—that was like a fucking bone in my throat—"Can we still be friends?" That's gotta be the stupidest question in the English language. (*AARON laughs ruefully*) Then we screwed one last time. For the road. Yeah and I screwed extra hard—to situate myself for the inevitable comparisons, you know. Then we said goodbye. At first, I was alright. The poison hadn't hit yet. I got myself a huge meal at this Chinese place—Just me and the newspaper. That's one of my favorite things in the world. Good food and *The New York Post*. It didn't work for me. I was feeling really violent that night. Like "How dare she leave me? I saved her fucking life!" I was really looking forward to the Tyson fight. Tyson was my boy, he'd put the world straight. We were born two days apart, same year, same hospital. Coulda been in the nursery together. I wanted to be vicious and invincible, just like him, blasting my way to the top. He was the youngest heavyweight champion of all time, I wanted to be the youngest billionaire C.E.O. or some shit. I watched the fight at the Full Moon Saloon. When I'm sad, I like to be with the poor, I don't know why. Did you see the fight? Douglas put him down, the whole bar was going fucking crazy. Mike was on his knees, trying to put his mouthpiece back in. You're right, he looked like a lost little boy. I don't care, once you see a man on his knees, he ain't never the same. Watching Tyson on the canvas, I was like, "Aaron, who are you kidding?" Watching Tyson on the canvas, all my dreams suddenly seemed ridiculous. I know this sounds funny, but I knew I was gonna die someday... (*pause*) This toothless black hag behind me starts screaming, "It was her that did it to him! It was that bitch, Robin Givens! That bitch did it to him!" That bitch, I said to myself, did it to me. I was a fucking mess, putting away more drinks. Then something funny happened, well not really funny, but... Well, yeah, it's funny, I guess... (*AARON starts laughing nervously*) I'm walking home, my head whirlin' from the whiskey and all that Chinese food I ate is working on my stomach. I hadda go to the bathroom so bad. I was doing that run skip, holding my ass tight. (*He starts to laugh harder*) I'm thinking, "I'm not gonna make it." So I'm finally in the elevator with Mrs. Lefkowitz and her poodle and I'm...I can't tell you this, Dad, fuck it— (*AARON and GIL are laughing uproariously*) I felt like a bad little boy, like "uh-oh"— (*This provokes fresh peals of laughter. AARON calms his laughter down so he can continue his story*) So I strip down, wash up, take the shitty underwear and wrap it in newspaper and put it all in a Gristedes bag. I'm too tired to go downstairs, I'm thinking, "What am I gonna do with this bag of shit?" (*His laugh fades completely. There is a silence*) I got this sudden pain in my chest, Dad, like someone put a pin in there maybe. "Broken heart," I thought that was just an expression. I couldn't get my breath and I started feeling that blackness you were talking about, thinking about other guys touching her and I...called her. 4:30 a.m. I said,

"Emily, I'm hurtin' here, can you come over?" She mumbled something. I said, "Is somebody there with you?" She didn't answer me, but I heard somebody back there. I said, "You gotta help me, Em, I'm asking as a friend, come over and be with me..." I'm crying in gasps—"I'm sorry, Aaron, I have nothing to give you right now." And I'm left there alone, with this big bag full of shit. Totally empty inside. I gave her that thing you should never give anybody. Here... (*He presses between his ribs, into his solar plexus*) That little extra you save for emergencies... (*pause*) So I throw the bag out the back window, only I hear this thud. It lands on the ledge outside Mrs. Cantor's apartment, one floor down. Can you believe that? I knew she'd find it the next morning when she was watering her plants. (*He laughs weakly*) So I take a broom and lean out the window. I try to knock the bag down into the alley, but I couldn't reach the fucking thing. I almost fell, almost... Finally, I throw the broom and hit it, send the thing flying... I'm watching it fall, it's about sixty feet to the concrete, the rats and garbage and graffiti and my heart's boomin' and my thoughts are driving me crazy. Suddenly, I wanted to be down there, too. I thought, "Iron Mike Tyson, how we gonna make it through the night?" He lost his title and his wife. I knew he was alone somewhere, hurtin' as bad as me. I closed my eyes and got both my feet on the window ledge, I was squatting there like a catcher. I was gonna jump... I don't know... Luckily, Mom sensed something. She caught me just in time.

OLEANNA by David Mamet

You can call it a riff on the Anita Hill-Clarence Thomas controversy or a particularly virulent battle in the war between men and women, but *Oleanna* is deceptively simple in plot and only becomes complicated when you try to figure out exactly what happened. A lot is said, but a lot more is insinuated and even more is to be discussed and argued about.

Here's what happens on paper: Carol, a student, has come to JOHN, a forty-year-old teacher, because she is failing his course. In between talking to his wife about the house they are buying and worrying about whether he will get tenure, John tries to soothe Carol and find out how to help her.

He is by turns concerned and anxious to get rid of her. They never reach an understanding about her work in the course as the first act ends.

Now, as Act Two begins, sometime later in the school year, John has discovered that Carol has reported him to the tenure committe as an elitist, sexist, purveyor of pornographic stories, and a physical harasser to boot. Eventually, she will raise the charge of attempted rape. John now tries to justify his decisions to Carol in an attempt to save his career.

SCENE: John's office

TIME: The present.

JOHN: You see, (*pause*) I love to teach. And flatter myself I am *skilled* at it. And I love the, the aspect of performance. I think I must confess that.

When I found I loved to teach I swore that I would not become that cold, rigid automaton of an instructor which I had encountered as a child.

Now, I was not unconscious that it was given me to err upon the other side. And, so, I asked and *ask* myself if I engaged in heterodoxy, I will not say "gratuitously" for I do not care to posit orthodoxy as a given good—but, "to the detriment of, of my students." (*Pause*)

As I said. When the possibility of tenure opened, and, of course, I'd long pursued it, I was, of course *happy*, and *covetous* of it.

I asked myself if I was wrong to covet it. And thought about it long, and, I hope, truthfully, and saw in myself several things in, I think, no particular order. (*Pause*)

That I *would* pursue it. That I *desired* it, that I was not pure of longing for security, and that that, perhaps, was not reprehensible in me. That I had duties beyond the school, and that my duty to my home, for instance, was, or should be, if it were not, of an equal weight. That tenure, and security, and yes, and *comfort*, were not, of themselves, to be scorned; and were even worthy of honorable pursuit. And that it was given me. Here, in this place, which I enjoy, and in which I find comfort, to assure myself of—as far as it rests in The Material—a continuation of that joy and comfort. In exchange for what? Teaching. Which I love.

What was the price of this security? To obtain tenure. Which tenure the committee is in the process of granting me. And on the basis of which I contracted to purchase a house. Now, as you don't have your own family, at this point, you may not know what that means. But to me it is important. A home. A Good Home. To raise my family. Now: The Tenure Committee will meet. This is the process, and a *good* process. Under which the school has functioned for quite a long time. They will meet, and hear your complaint—which you have the right to make; and they will dismiss it. They will dismiss your complaint; and, in the intervening period, I will lose my house. I will not be able to close on my house. I will lose my deposit, and the home I'd picked out for my wife and son will go by the boards. Now: I see I have angered you. I understand your anger at teachers. I was angry with mine. I felt hurt and humiliated by them. Which is one of the reasons that I went into education. [CAROL: What do you want of me?] (*Pause*) I was hurt. When I received the report. Of the tenure committee. I was shocked. And I was hurt. No, I don't mean to subject you to my weak sensibilities. All right. Finally, I didn't understand. Then I thought: is it not always at those points at which we reckon ourselves unassailable that we are most vulnerable and... (*Pause*) Yes. All right. You find me pedantic. Yes. I am. By nature, by birth, by profession, I don't know.

ON FORGETTING by John Pielmeier

An ACTOR speaks.

SCENE: An empty stage during the performance of *On Forgetting*.

TIME: The present.

An empty stage.
The ACTOR enters, breathing heavily. There is a trickle of blood on his forehead.
ACTOR: I remember when I was twelve I saw this movie about a guy who was hit on the head with a brick, he was walking down the street and a pigeon knocked this brick off the edge of this old building

and it fell and hit him on the head and when he woke up he couldn't remember who he was or who he was married to or anything and he wandered all over the city looking for clues, and each day he forgot a little more, like what country this was or how to add and subtract, and on Tuesday he forgot how to tie his shoes, and on Friday he walked out into the street and blam, he was hit by a car cause he forgot to look. And he lay in the street, looking up to heaven and the crowd of people around him staring down, and his last words were...

Um.

It'll come to me.

Let me start over.

In my dressing room there's this water pipe separating the men's side from the women's side, and the toilet is on the women's side and this pipe is very low because the room wasn't supposed to be a dressing room to begin with, the people who built the building didn't think, well we'll put the dressing room here, they thought it would be a _____ building or something, people wouldn't need dressing rooms, and I had to go to the bathroom, and I heard my cue, and I thought I could make it if I ran and I ran right into that water pipe about a minute and a half ago—you can feel the bump right here—and, um...

(*He notices the blood on his forehead and wipes it off with his hand.*)
It would be a terrible thing to forget who you are. I was born on...

(*The ACTOR quickly tells us four or five things, true or false, one infinitely sad and one very unlikeable, all very brief, about himself.*)

It's important for me to remember these things because it helps me forget that in a hundred years nobody will remember, or care to, unless I do something like (*The ACTOR names something important he has done or some role he has played, something the audience may remember.*) in which case everyone will remember me, especially schoolkids who get a day off to celebrate (*ACTOR's name*)'s Birthday, but this is all very unlikely, in a hundred years I'll be dust or ashes or atomic rubble, and so will you, we'll all be forgotten except as a kind of representative mass of 19—, or in a thousand years of the twentieth century, or maybe even of the Planet Earth, we'll all be grouped with Shakespeare or Jesus, if anyone remembers who *they* are—forgetting is the cornerstone of annihilation, and in this business it's worse

90

because we make our money by remembering what to say next and if I forget then (*Director's name*) will fire my ass.

So how do I remember all these lines? I go over them again and again and again and again, and that line is easy to remember because it has four agains in it, all I have to do is remember four, but if I'm nervous or hit on the head I may forget to count, or I may remember three or five, which is no big deal you say, like you don't know or care if I am delivering this speech word perfect, but John Pielmeier cares, and he could be tearing out his hair at this very moment because I just remembered that there *are* five agains, and I only said four...I think...

I go over them again and again and again and again, and again, and then I'll try to do it without the page in front of me, and then I'll look at it and check it, and then I'll try to do a larger clump, and the word *clump* is important because I used to say hunk, and I used to say I'll look at it and check it *again,* I added another again and I shouldn't have, and if you think about it, even the words I'm saying to you now, even though they're going by so quickly, I spent hours on each word, it is so important that I say every word, *each* word, it is so important that I say *each* word precisely as it was conceived because every slip of the mind is a little nudge toward death, and when I'm word perfect, after many hours, I'll bring it into rehearsal and forget most of everything, it's a little bit like Hell, I think, and when I get it right I'll run to come out on stage because I almost forgot my cue and I'll hit my head on a pipe and it's all up for grabs, the speech, the evening, my job, me.

His dying words were so important.

I think.

(*There is a long uncomfortable pause. The STAGE MANAGER talks over the house speaker.*)

[STAGE MANAGER: You want a line?]

I don't know.

[STAGE MANAGER: And he lay in the street looking up to heaven...]

...and the crowd of people around him staring down, and his last words were... (*A long pause. The ACTOR fights his tears...*) I'm sorry. (*...and walks off the stage.*)

91

ON THE OPEN ROAD by Steve Tesich

Two men—ANGEL (in his twenties) and Al—join forces to make their way to the "Land of the Free." Al has a cartful of great works of art he's using to negotiate their way into freedom.

Using a pulley and rope, Angel lifts a beautiful statue into his cart. He explains how the Civil War began.

SCENE: Inside a large bombed-out museum.

TIME: The future, in a period of civil war.

Out of the darkness, a ray of light illuminates a large beautiful statue. The statue is still for a beat or so and then it begins to rise up. More light. We now see that we're inside a large bombed-out museum. A thick, nylon rope is attached to the statue. The rope is draped over a high steel beam overhead, exposed by the bombing. Using a pulley, ANGEL is lifting the statue off the ground. The cart is not far away. AL has taken off the tarp and is now taking out some paintings that we can't see. He is stacking them on the ground to make room for the statue. More light. We see little pyramids of dead bodies here and there. Corridors radiating in three directions. ANGEL grunts as he works. Despite the pulley, it's hard work lifting up the statue. When it's high enough, AL will position the cart to receive the statue and ANGEL will lower it. Once in the cart, AL will wedge in the paintings around it and ANGEL will disassemble the pulley and put the rope and the pulley in the cart and AL will then place the tarp over the whole thing and the cart will be ready to go. All this will take place during ANGEL's monologue.

ANGEL: If I was God, I'd change some things in the Bible. About how you shouldn't make graven images of God. If I was God, I wouldn't give a shit if they made graven images of me. What do I care? I'm God. Can't hurt me to be graven. Nothing can hurt me. I'm God. But I would put in its place, in big letters: Thou shalt not make graven images of your fellow man.

(He pauses to rest a bit.)

The very first time I ever went to a museum was right before the Civil War broke out.

(Continues to work.)

It was one of those scum-of-the-earth days at the museum. If you're scum, you get in free. These social agencies rounded us up and took us there in school buses. About three hundred of us. Young scum. Old scum. Half-way house scum. No-house scum. A cross-section. It was in order to uplift us they took us there. I was delighted to be in that air-conditioned place. That by itself was uplifting enough for me.

(The statue is now high enough. Al moves the cart under it. Angel lowers it slowly, as Al guides it.)

But there was this exhibit there in the museum. These artworks of a contemporary nature. And every work of art showed some man or woman or kid who was having a real bad time of it. Street-type sufferers and the like. We're snickering among ourselves in that stupid scum-of-the-earth way of ours. What? We came all the way here to see more scum like us. But the others, the regular people, in chic lightweight summer suits and dresses with brochures in their hands, they're not snickering at all. And they're offended 'cause we are. They are seriously moved by what they see in the exhibit. They are telling each other how beautiful it all is, this exhibit of human suffering. I try to ignore them, but it was like the air-conditioning broke down or something, 'cause I start feeling hot. It's rubbing me all wrong to hear about the beauty of it all. Not that far from the museum, twenty blocks or so uptown where I lived, there was the same kind of exhibit. Same kind of suffering. Only it wasn't beautiful there. And there were no couples in chic lightweight summer clothes to be moved by it all. What was fucking scum-of-the-earth outside the museum was a fucking masterpiece inside. And then this thing starts crawling through my brain. This really painful idea that maybe there was something in me worth seeing, that nobody would ever see so long as these artworks were there. I know what I'm thinking, but I'm trying not to think it, 'cause it's no good thinking such thoughts. But then I hear it. It's like I hear the other scum-of-the-earth there thinking the same thing. And suddenly it's a much bigger thought. It's like ants. I read in this nature magazine once that ants don't have brains and that ants don't talk unless there's enough of them that get together. Two ants got nothing to say to each other. They don't know what to do. But if a few hundred of them get together, a brain is born. Suddenly, we started trashing it all. Breaking up statues and tearing the paintings to shreds. There were these armed guards there and they shot a bunch of us, but we didn't care. Ants don't really care if a bunch gets killed. We set fire to the museum and ran out into the street.

(*The cart is loaded. The tarp is over the cart. The ladder now hangs from some pegs on its side.*)

[AL: And so another Civil War began.]

For once I was there at the start of something. It was very pleasant to realize you didn't really have to be highly qualified to make history.

OTHER PEOPLE'S MONEY by Jerry Sterner

LAWRENCE GARFINKLE, an obese, cunning New York "take over" artist, about forty, has been buying up shares of the old-line and undervalued New England Wire and Cable Company. He has one goal—to gain control of the cable company, dismantle it, and make a huge profit. His success in similar ventures has earned him the nickname "Larry the Liquidator."

In the final scenes of the play, Garfinkle must persuade the stockholders to vote in his slate of board members to carry out his plans. He follows the Chief Executive of the company who has pleaded for the retention of the old board and the American values of business it represents.

SCENE: Podium at stockholders meeting. Rhode Island.

TIME: The present.

GARFINKLE: Amen...And Amen...And Amen. Say "Amen," someone, please! (*Moves to lectern and says in a hushed tone.*) You'll excuse me. I'm not familiar with local custom...The way I was brought up you always said "Amen" after you heard a prayer. You hear someone praying, after he finishes, you say "Amen" and drink a little wine.

'Cause that's what you just heard—a prayer. The way I was brought up we called the particular prayer "the prayer for the dead." You just heard the prayer for the dead, and, fellow stuckholders, you didn't say "Amen" and you didn't even get to sip the wine.

What—You don't think this company is dead? Steel—you remember steel, don't you? Steel used to be an industry. Now heavy metal is a rock group.

This company is dead. Don't blame me. I didn't kill it. It was dead when I got here. It is too late for prayers, for even if the prayers were answered and a miracle occurred and the yen did this and the dollar did that and the infrastructure did the other thing, we would still be dead. Know why? Fiber-optics. New technologies. Obsolescence.

We're dead, all right. We're just not broke. And you know the surest way to go broke? Keep getting an increasing share of a shrinking market. Down the tubes. Slow but sure. You know, at one time there must have been dozens of companies making buggy whips. And I'll bet you anything the last one around was the one that made the best goddamned buggy whip you ever saw. How would you have liked to have been a stuckholder of that company?

You invested in a business. And that business is dead. Let's have the intelligence, let's have the decency, to sign the death certificate, collect the insurance and invest the money in something with a future.

Aha—But we can't, goes the prayer—we can't because we have a responsibility—a responsibility to our employees, our community...What will happen to them? I got words for that—"Who cares?" Care about them? They didn't care about you. They sucked you dry. You have no responsibility to them.

For the last ten years this company has bled your money. Did this Community care? Did they ever say, "I know things are tough. We'll lower your taxes, reduce water and sewer?" Check it out. We're paying twice what we paid ten years ago.

And the mayor is making twice what he made ten years ago. And our devoted employees, after taking no increases for three years, are still making twice what they made ten years ago. And our stock is one-sixth what it was ten years ago. Who cares? I'll tell you—me! I'm not your best friend—I'm your only friend. I care about you in the only way that matters in business. I don't make anything? I'm making you

95

money. And, lest we forget, that's the only reason any of you became stuckholders in the first place. To make money. You don't care if they manufacture wire and cable, fry chicken, or grow tangerines. You want to make money. I'm making you money. I'm the only friend you got.

Take that money. Invest it somewhere else. Maybe—maybe you'll get lucky and it will be used productively—and if it is—you'll create more jobs and provide a service for the economy and—God forbid—even make a few bucks for yourself. Let the Government and the Mayor and the unions worry about what you paid them to worry about. And if anyone asks, tell them you gave at the plant.

And it pleases me that I'm called "Larry the Liquidator." You know why, fellow stuckholders? Because at my funeral you'll leave with a smile on your face...and a few bucks in your pocket. Now, that's a funeral worth having. (*Breathing heavily, GARFINKLE pauses a beat and sits.*)

OUT THE WINDOW by Neal Bell

JAKE, a man in his twenties, experiences a rude awakening.

SCENE: The kitchen of a New York apartment.

TIME: The present.

A kitchen. Early morning light from the windows over the sink.

Up high, on top of the kitchen table, a wheelchair. In the wheelchair, JAKE, in his twenties, is sprawled, completely out. He's wearing a wildly disheveled tux. In one dangling hand he clutches an empty bottle. JAKE is loudly sawing wood.

The bottle slips from his hand and hits the floor, with a CRASH that troubles Jake's sleep.

JAKE: (*Eyes closed.*) WHO'S THERE? (*He reacts to his shout.*) Oww! Jeez Louise, let me try that again, little softer: Who's there? Andy? (*He feels the surrounding air with his hands.*) Nothing. Me and my chair.

(*Far off a COCK crows.*)

Hit the snooze-alarm on that rooster, would you? I'm up. Well, almost up. And I'd open my eyes, to greet the day and you, but I'm guessing that light would not be what the doctor ordered, and speaking of tongue and spirit depressors...One of my sweat-socks passed away in my mouth, could you bring me a glass of water, see if I can just flush the sucker, yo, Andrea, hey, little help...

(Again the off-stage ROOSTER crows. JAKE winces.)
And could somebody kindly get the hook for that bird?
(The ROOSTER crows.)

Do I live on a farm? Survey SAYS...*(He buzzes "no.")* OK, did I go to a party so trendy that animal acts were a part of the entertainment? Survey SAYS...I don't remember. Much about that party. At all. I recall a taxi-ride through the Park. And then a mahogany elevator. And then a lot of Republicans. People who *looked* like Republicans, anyway, bow-ties flapping away...and then you wheeling me out of the madding crowd, and into the dark and onto your bed, *somebody's* bed, whosever bed the party was, and the rest is the kind of history you're condemned to repeat...which I wouldn't mind, repeating, except next time, Andrea, sweetie, baby, doll, I'd like to remember. The way you feel. The way you taste. The way you move. For both of us. Remember all that, and not black out and be shovelled back into my chair, like a sack of sheep-dip, and shoved out into the hall or wherever I am, stark raving alone, if I *am* alone, if I open my eyes...if I open my eyes and you've slunk away— Andrea?...I'm going to feel, fair warning here, very crippled up and very done in by Life, as I know it now, and extremely very sorry I ever was born, it is going to get *that* ugly and whiny and borderline-truly-obnoxious, I swear, so be it on your delectable head, if I open my eyes... *(He opens his eyes.)* Andrea? *(He looks around.)* So you slopped me back in my chair after all, and abandoned me halfway up the kitchen...wall... *(He looks down, suddenly realizing his chair is up in the air, on a table.)* ...and screw a Mallard. I'm up on a table. *(Pause.)* Screw a green and yellow Mallard sideways. How'd I...like a giant entree, defrosting. How'd I get up on a table?

PARTY TIME by Harold Pinter

A group of wealthy socialites drink and discuss the opening of a new health club. TERRY is a man of forty.

SCENE: A large room. Sofas, armchair, etc. People sitting, standing. A waiter with a drink tray. Spasmodic party music throughout the play.

TIME: The present.

The lights in the room dim.

The light beyond the open door gradually intensifies. It burns into the room.

The door light fades down. The room lights come up on TERRY, DUSTY, GAVIN, MELISSA, FRED, CHARLOTTE, DOUGLAS, and LIZ.

TERRY: The thing is, it is actually real value for money. Now this is a very, very unusual thing. It is an extremely unusual thing these days to find that you are getting real value for money. You take your hand out of your pocket and you put your money down and you know what you're getting. And what you're getting is absolutely gold-plated service. Gold-plated service in all departments. You've got real catering. You've got catering on all levels. You've not only got very good catering in itself—you know, food, that kind of thing—and napkins—you know, all that, wonderful, first rate—but you've also got artistic catering—you actually have an atmosphere—in this club— which is catering artistically for its clientele. I'm refering to the kind of light, the kind of paint, the kind of music, the club offers. I'm talking about a truly warm and harmonious environment. You won't find voices raised in our club. People don't do vulgar and sordid and offensive things. And if they do we kick them down the stairs with no trouble at all.

THE PHONE MAN by Craig Lucas

A self-contained monologue for an unspecified speaker.

SCENE: A pier in New York.

TIME: The present.

I loved this guy who worked for the phone company. He told me what he did there, but I can't remember. I think he worked out at my gym. I think that's where we met. I loved his flattened nose—like those guys in those old obscene drawings with the crew cuts and rolledup sleeves and thick lips and tattoos. Every one of 'em has the same dumb fuck-me eyes. This guy didn't have a tattoo, but he had a mild, sweet version of all the rest.

I'll tell you who had a tattoo, though—a really beautiful orange and blue one of a bird—was my friend Geoff who I know I met at the gym. I think we had sex twice. He was a dream. What a handsome easy-going guy, all of maybe five foot six. He worked as a bellhop in one of the new hotels while he studied to be an actor. Then I heard he was in a movie. And I saw it. He was pretty good, too. He once asked me if I would fuck him. He was nervous about it, he said, because he'd never done it. He didn't say it like it was a line either. But maybe it was. I wrote a part for him in a movie and even called the character Geoff, but the real one was sick by then and couldn't do it. No, that's not right. He'd already died the week before we called to offer him the part. It wound up getting cut from the movie anyway. The guy who did play it is dead too. His room just sent me a Christmas card with the news. He had lesions on his face when we shot his scenes, but he'd cover them up with make-up. I wonder about my friend Geoff, though. I loved fucking him, but I wonder if that's what got him going, looking for other guys to fuck him without a rubber. This was before we knew, wasn't it? Or when we knew and didn't want to know—that little sliver of time between hearing and knowing. No, I think it was before. *Right* before.

But the guy from the phone company. God, I loved making love to him. We didn't fuck. I don't think he was into it. That's probably why I still used to see him around in the mid-80's—maybe once or twice, that's all. He wouldn't acknowledge me. Do I look so old? Did I stop returning his calls? Did I want to pretend I never stood naked on

99

the roof of the pier with my dick in and out of two mouths, liking that people were looking, admiring it with its smooth head like a shiny purple stone? But I loved the telephone man's cock. It wasn't real big but it was straight forward and kind of blunt like his nose and his forehead. I think of him as a Neanderthal with nice manners—the kind of daddy your well-behaved friends had when you were in kindergarten.

Imagine if all the nice daddies died. Imagine if they got sick from a virus spread in steak and potatoes or from having to carry an attache case to and from work on the commuter train. Or maybe it was the air inside the train that killed them. But surely they were innocent and they didn't give it to one another in an act of love or friendship like shaking hands or doing business. That would be inexcusable, wouldn't it? If they gave it to their kids when they kissed them, when they were so overcome with love and pride and having to clutch each one to their breasts and plant a loving, deadly kiss to their warm, flushed faces.

I loved that guy from the phone company. God, I hope he's alive. Why can't I remember his name?

A POSTER OF THE COSMOS by Lanford Wilson

TOM, a large brooding man of thirty-six, is being questioned by the police about how he met his flatmate, Johnny. Tom is a baker and Johnny works in a hospital, ordering and picking up supplies.

SCENE: A police station in New York City.

TIME: 1987.

TOM: So, I get off work at seven, I'm eatin' at this place I always did, Johnny's havin' breakfast. He's depressed 'cause the Cosmos folded. Soccer team. I think they'd folded about five years back but he'd got to thinkin' about it again. And we're talkin' about atmospheric pressure, which is something it happens I've read a lot about, and we're both readers that only read factual stuff. Only I read slow and forget it and he reads like tearin' through things and remembers. And we'd both been married when we was kids, and had a kid of our own, only, you know, it turned out he didn't. And he said he was gay now and he'd been like fuckin' everythin' in sight for five years only he'd got frustrated with it and hadn't been laid in a month, and we're bitchin' our jobs and he got up and goes off for a minute and comes back and says why don't we go around the corner to his apartment 'cause we're takin' up two seats at the counter and this is a business based on volume and I said, no, you got to go to work and he said…"I just called in sick." (*He smiles, then thinks about it. A frown, a troubled pause.*) That's funny. He really did, first time I met him, called in sick. I never thought about that—till right now. (*Beat.*) Jesus, all that talkin' about food makes me realize I ain't eaten in two days. (*A beat. He looks at the cops expectantly. Apparently there is no reaction.*) Fuck it, skip it. So anyway, if you'da said I'd be livin' wid a guy I'da said, you know, go fuck yourself. And it stayed like that. It was somethin' that always surprised me, you know? Well, of course you don't. Assholes. But I'd wake up, go in the livin' room, he'd be in a chair or somethin', you know, twitchin' like he was deliverin' somethin' somewhere. Or actually sometimes he'd be in bed there. And it always like surprised me. I'd think, what the hell do you know about this? If he'd been like a big old hairy guy or something probably nothing would have happened, but Johnny didn't have hair on his body, he had like this peach fuzz all over him that made him feel like…skip it. I'm your kinna guy, right? I don't think. I don't analyze. So you know…we had like…three years. We did go down to St. Pete. He'd heard about it, he'd always wanted to go. We didn't like it. We went on down to Key West, he'd heard about that, too. That was worse. We come back, rented a car, went up to Vermont. And that was good. Except for Johnny drivin', I couldn't let him drive 'cause he'd go crazy. We'd get behind a tractor or somethin', he'd go ape. Also I'd get dizzy on the roads all up and down and curvin' and Johnny being this like aerobic driver. (*Pause.*) So after three years, when he started gettin' sick…they was very good about it at the hospital. They let him come to work for a while. Then, you know, like I said, he'd dig at himself and bleed, so that wasn't possible. That'd be real bad. So then I started being the one that was crazy all the time and I'd get off and come home in the morning, he'd be starin' out the window or somethin'. He'd say, "I slept fourteen hours." It was like this blessing for him; like this miracle, he couldn't believe it. I guess everything that was goin' on in him, I guess was interesting to him. He was like studying it. I'd say, "What?" And he'd hold up his hand for me to be quiet for a long time and then he'd say, "I'd never have believed pain could be that bad. This is amazing." You know, he had like his intestines all eaten out and that and he had insurance and the hospital was good to him. They all visited him, but he didn't take the painkillers. He was curious about it. (*He looks around, then goes on rather flatly.*) Then he got worse and started takin' 'em. (*Beat.*) You could see by his expression that he hadn't thought he was gonna do that. The staff, the nurses and you know, the volunteers, the ghouls that get off on that, they were okay. They didn't get in our way much. (*Searching, becoming frustrated.*) What I couldn't believe was that I didn't have it. I got the fuckin' test, it was negative. I couldn't believe that. Twice. I couldn't figger that, 'cause like the first time I was with him, I just fucked him and he like laid up against me and jerked off. And that was sorta what we did for a while. That was our pattern; you know, you fall into routines. But after a while, you get familiar with someone, I was all over him. No way I wasn't exposed to that like three times a week for three years. What the hell was goin' on? I got to thinkin' maybe he didn't have it, maybe it was somethin' else, but... (*He settles down, pauses, thinks of something else.*) He had these friends at the hospital, offered him somethin', I don't know what, take him out of his misery, he didn't take it, he wanted to see it through to the end like. (*A little frustration creeps back.*) See, my problem was I didn't really know what he was goin' through. You help and you watch and it tears you up, sure, but you don't know *what,* you know, whatta you know? (*Beat.*) He wanted to come home, but...uh... (*Pause. He regards the cops.*) This is the only part you fucks care about, so listen up. We wanted him to be home for the end, but it slipped up on us. We thought he'd come home another time but he went into this like semicoma and just went right outta sight, he just sank. I didn't know if he recognized me or not. I got this old poster of the Cosmos and put it up on the wall across from the bed. They had him propped up in bed, but he just looked scared. He saw it and he said, "What's that?" You know, you know you know everythin' in the room and it's all familiar, and he hadn't seen that before. Probably it was just this big dark thing in front of him that he couldn't tell what it was and it scared him. He didn't understand it. (*Looking around.*) This gets bloody, so if you're faint of heart or anything. (*Looking up.*) All you fuckers out in TV land, recordin' this shit for fuckin' posterity; check your focus, this is hot shit, they're gonna wanna know this. (*Pause.*) So the nurse comes by, I said he's restin'. She was glad to skip him. And I took off my clothes and held him. He was sayin', it sounded like, "This is curious." And there was just like nothin' to him. (*Pause.*) See the problem is, like I said, I was the one who was crazy now. And, uh, well, to hell with it. I'm your kinna guy, fellas, I won't think about it. We do what we do, we do what's gotta be done. (*And rather coldly, or that is what he tries for.*) So he died in my arms and I held him a long time and then I cut a place on his cheek where he used to dig and on his chest where he used to gouge out these red marks and in his hair. And when the blood came I licked it off him. Cleaned him up. So then the nurse come, you know, and shit a brick and called you guys. But they let me hold him till you come. I guess they was afraid of me. Or maybe of all the blood. Then they knew I had to be crazy, 'cause like we agreed, I'm not the kinna guy'd do somethin' like dat. What they thought, I think, was that I'd killed him, but that wasn't what he wanted and what I had to consider now was myself. And what I wanted. (*Pause.*) So if it don't take again, then I'm like fucked, which wouldn't be the first time. I guess there's gonna be maybe some compensation in knowin' I did what I could. (*A long wandering pause, then he looks at them.*) So. Are you happy now? (*A pause. Eight counts.*)

ROAD TO NIRVANA by Arthur Kopit

JERRY, a man in his forties, used to be in the film biz. He has a chance to produce the film of Nirvana's (read: Madonna's) life story. He's had to literally eat excrement to prove himself worthy. Now, the rock star wants him to cut off a testicle for her. Lou, one of his partners, criticizes him for hesitating. Jerry takes umbrage.

SCENE: Nirvana's estate—a kind of pagan temple with a grand staircase. Los Angeles.

TIME: The present.

JERRY: Who the fuck are you to talk to me like that? What the fuck do *you* know about what I've been through? And I don't mean just today either, I mean in my life, my LIFE! All right? Okay? So *FUCK OFF!* I mean what the fuck are *you* giving up for this, a tit? I don't see you giving up SHIT for this! This is not an easy thing this woman's asking me to do, not easy, not at all, by no *STRETCH OF THE IMAGINATION* is this an easy thing to do! Or do you think it is?...I mean, you think I'm just gonna say "Here honey? Sure, please, feel free, take 'em! And while you're at it, take anything else you want—take my fingers, take my ears." FUCK YOU! *You* get out of here! *YOUUUUUUU* get out o' here! 'Cause I'm not moving. (*Pointing to NIRVANA.*) If she wants me out, I will go. Not you, not Al, *she*...gives the word to me around this place, not you. (*Turning to NIRVANA.*) I'm in. [LOU: Bullshit.] Yeah? Fuck you bullshit! You're the one who's bullshit! You and Al. I'm the one she needs. You understand me? *Needs.* We have a connection you will never have. *Never!* (*Turning to NIRVANA—strong, resolute.*) You want two? Say the word and I will give you two. I will. I mean if that is what you want, really truly want, two it is, two it fuckin' is! Which is not to say I wouldn't much prefer giving none. I would. I mean, hey, you think I'm crazy? Of COURSE I would! Or, in a pinch, just one. Of course I would. *But!* Here's the point: if two is what it takes to make you know that I'm with you, come what may, for better or for worse, two it is, two it fuckin' is. And I will leave this decision entirely to you. You say you need to know you can trust in me? Well I will trust in you. In your judgment and your goodness. 'Cause you know what?—the gods did not send me to you. They sent you to me! This film is going to set clocks ticking in a whole new fuckin' direction. This film is going to make fuckin' HISTORY! And I am going to be part of it! (*To Lou and Al, with controlled ferocity.*) And no one's going to fuckin' stop me. NO ONE! "MOBY FUCKIN' DICK!" Melville *knew* where his book would lead, he fuckin' *KNEW!* (*Stunned—a sudden revelation.*) *That's why he wrote the book!* (*To Nirvana, with steely calm, confident as hell.*) Where's the operating room?

104

ROSE COTTAGES by Bill Bozzone

LYDELL, white, seventeen, and a runaway, has found work with Rose, the black owner of a ramshackle motel. The relationship vacillates betweeen explosive hate and grudging acceptance. When Rose suggests that Lydell try to talk things over with his hated father, the boy replies.

SCENE: The exterior of Rose Cottages, just outside Orlando, Florida. A rickety porch leads to one of the four cottages.

TIME: The present.

LYDELL: Here's the way it was. (*beat*) Christmas Eve, nineteen-seventy...I forget. (*ROSE looks straight up—a gesture for LYDELL to "get on with it."*) With the snow coming down just like in the movies. [ROSE: I ain't getting no younger here, boy.] I'm only five years old, Rose. [ROSE: Five years old.] My father—the man you want me to talk things out with—is sitting in the living room reading a dirty book. All I want to know is when's Santa Claus coming. So I keep asking him. "When's Santa Claus coming? When's Santa Claus coming?" [ROSE: That could annoy the shit out of anybody, Lydell.] He's hardly even listening to me! (*pause*) Anyway, he always used to keep this gun by the arm of his chair. This old .45. He was convinced that some heavy drug user was gonna come in, right through the front door. He wanted to be ready. (*pause*) So I'm asking him. "When's Santa Claus coming?" And all of a sudden he just throws his book down, right? He grabs this .45. And the next thing I know, he opens the front door and runs outside. (*pause*) I hear a shot. [ROSE: He killed himself.] How could he kill himself? He's still alive. I told you that. [ROSE: (*short pause*) Go ahead.] He comes back inside. (*short pause*) He sits, he picks up his book, he puts the gun down...(*short pause*) And he says to me...Rose...he says to me. "He's dead. The Santa Claus is dead. He's not coming. I shot the goddamn Santa Claus." [ROSE: You bullshittin'.] Nope. [ROSE: He shot the goddamn Santa Claus?] That what he said. (*A moment of silence. ROSE, slowly at first, begins to chuckle.*) You think that's funny? (*ROSE laughs harder.*) It's very damaging to a kid, Rose! (*ROSE is close to tears-of-laughter. LYDELL, fighting unsuccessfully, begins to laugh along.*) And that's not even the best part. [ROSE: (*laughing*) No more!] (*laughing*) The best part is, that Christmas I didn't get all I wanted, so I figured the old man just "winged" him.

ROSE COTTAGES by Bill Bozzone

LYDELL, white, seventeen, and a runaway, has found work with Rose, the black owner of a ramshackle motel. Their relationship vacillates betweeen explosive hate and grudging acceptance.

While trying to fix an air conditioner for one of his guests, Rose causes a short which sends an electric shock through the woman, knockingher unconscious. Rose makes Lydell stay with the woman while he goes for spirits to revive her. Lydell tries to make comforting conversation with the guest.

SCENE: The exterior of Rose Cottages, just outside Orlando, Florida. A rickety porch leads to one of the four cottages.

TIME: The present.

LYDELL: So. You feel like a little TV? (*He rises, turns the set on, changes the channels.*) You're gonna be fine, no kidding. We'll laugh about this someday. Really. The three of us. Rolling on the floor. (*The TV comes on. The theme from "Three's Company" plays.*) Here we go. You ever watch this? (*pause*) No? (*pause*) Well, it's a little complicated if you never watched it, but follow along with me. Okay? (*pause*) Okay. (*LYDELL sits on the side of the bed. He indicates the TV.*) Now this is not the show. This is the commercial. This is a guy who's not a doctor, but he plays one on TV. (*beat*) Makes it all right for him to sell medicine. (*LYDELL laughs. Pause.*) Hey. I'll tell you what. While we watch... (*LYDELL gets the cards from the table.*) we can play a little cards. A little poker. Would you like that? Sure. (*LYDELL returns to the bed, sits, deals.*) Jacks or better to open. They're coming out. (*He holds JESSIE'S card in front of her face.*)

Can you open? (*LYDELL looks at her cards.*) You got queens. Means you can open. I got...(*He looks at his own cards.*) Nothing. I fold. Queens win. (*short pause*) Another game? (*pause*) No? (*pause*) Fine. (*LYDELL puts the cards back on table, returns.*) We'll just watch a little TV. (*LYDELL watches a moment.*) Okay. Now I've seen this one before. I can fill you in. (*pause*) Now the landlord there thinks the kid there is...strange. Okay? But he's not. He's making believe. So that he can live with these two girls at once. (*pause*) Now I know what you're thinking. You think you know what he's after. Right? (*beat*) Wrong. (*beat*) He's not really interested in those girls. Not the way you're thinking. What he wants is for the landlord to find out for himself that this kid's all right. (*short pause*) Maybe they'll make friends and the landlord'll invite him down to his place. And that way they can all live together—the kid, the two girls, the landlord, his wife...Maybe they'll all wind up hanging out together. (*pause*) That'd be all right. (*pause*) Crowded, but all right. (*Long pause, then directly to JESSIE.*) You speak any foreign languages?

SALAAM, HUEY NEWTON, SALAAM by Ed Bullins

This play deals frankly and unsparingly with a generation of black leaders wasted by crack. One of them—who fell the farthest—Huey Newton, leader of the Black Panthers was once a model of black pride, action, and youth. Here is the last meeting between MARVIN X, in his forties, and his old friend, Huey, who used to live in penthouses but now scores crack in dirty Oakland school yards. Soon, HUEY will be dead.

SCENE: A street corner, West Oakland, California.

TIME: The present.

MARVIN: (*Smokes.*) Yeah...I tried to help him...but I couldn't...I couldn't help Huey because I was sick myself...The Bible says when the blind lead the blind, they both fall in the ditch together...The last time I saw Huey alive was in front of this same crack house here in West Oakland's infamous Acorn housing project, right next to the Cypress freeway that was devastated during the October 17, 1990 earthquake.

In 1984 I became addicted to crack cocaine...Many people, especially members of my family, found my addiction difficult to understand. "You're so strong," they would say. "How could you become a weak, pitiful dope fiend?" But I did...My addiction came in my fortieth year, for many people, a time of disillusionment with life, and certainly it was for me...I was burnt out...Tired of revolution, tired of family life, sex and women, tired of working in the educational system, tired of the black middle class and the grass roots, tired of religious sectarianism, Christian and Muslim alike, tired...

Maybe this is what happens when one lives too fast. You not only get burned out, but you run out of ideas...What mountain shall I conquer next?...And a voice came to me and said: "You shall become Sisyphus. You shall roll a rock up a mountain and it shall fall to earth, and you shall begin again each day for eternity, since you can't figure out anything else to do, you big dummy!"

So I was a sitting duck for an addiction, that is, a new addiction, especially when I became an entrepreneur and had large sums of cash on a daily basis. Yeah, I sold incense and perfume oils and lots of stuff on the street at Market and Powell in San Francisco. I made a lot of quick, easy money...And money added to my problems because I hated making money. I actually felt guilty about it and had to do something with all that money I had...So my friends, including my so-called Muslim brothers, introduced me to crack...I didn't like sniffing cocaine. For one reason, my mind is naturally speedy, so I did not want anything to speed it up more. I wanted to slow down, relax. My thing was weed. I admit, I abused weed because I smoked it from morning 'til night for over twenty years...My thing was weed, wine, and women. I always said I wanted to die from an overdose of weed, wine, and women, but along came crack and soon I had no desire for wine, weed, or women. With all my knowledge, I had forgotten the simple rules of life: for every blues, there is a happy song—sing a happy song—it takes the same energy as the blues...Even before my addiction to crack, why couldn't I think of all the good in my life? Why couldn't I sing songs of praise to Allah, my God, for the beautiful parents He had blessed me with, for my beautiful brothers and sisters, for the beautiful, intelligent women I had had, for the most beautiful children any man could imagine? Why? Why? Why?...Yes, I know now...because I thought I was self-sufficient.

I had sat and watched my friends smoking crack, but at first it didn't interest me. I did not like the way they behaved...I'd come into the room and they wouldn't even look up and acknowledge my presence. They were all staring at whoever had the pipe...But finally, the devil caught me, only because I forgot Allah. (*He chants.*)

I lost my wife behind the pipe
I lost my children behind the pipe
I lost my money behind the pipe
I lost my house behind the pipe
I lost my mind behind the pipe
I lost my life behind the pipe...

Yes, crack sent me to the mental hospital four times...Many times I put crack on my pipe and took that big 747 hit, and I could feel death coming, could feel my body surrounded by the strangest sensation. I would run to the window for air, or run outside for air. But after the moment of death had passed, I returned to my room and continued smoking...Once I accidentally cut my wrist, cut an artery. I dropped one of my pipes and grabbed at the broken pieces, cutting me critically, but I was unaware. I thought the bleeding would stop, but it didn't. I found my backup pipe and fired up...A friend tried to get me to go to the hospital, but I thought the blood would stop dripping from my wrist. It didn't. My new pipe became covered with blood. My dope had turned the color of blood. My clothes, the rug, the bed, the curtain, were all covered with blood. But I didn't stop. I kept on smoking...Finally, my friend got the hotel manager and he came in with a baseball bat and forced me out of the room...The paramedics came and took me to the hospital...Ha ha ha...after the emergency room crew stitched my wound, I got on the bus and returned to my room to finish smoking...Hell, I still had sixty bucks...fuck it!

SEARCH AND DESTROY by Howard Korder

Martin Mirheim, a would-be movie producer, decides to finance his picture through a cocaine deal. He is put in touch with a dealer named RON, who clearly partakes of the product he sells. Ron sings the praises of the Big Apple, from his unique viewpoint. He's talking about last night.

SCENE: A New York restaurant.

TIME: The present.

RON: The best. The best. Absofuckingwhatley the best. Last night. Okay. We get there. This is at Shea. We get there. In the limo. I got, I'm with, the, *Carol,* she does the, the, *fuck,* you know, that *ad,* the fitness, amazing bod, amazing bod, fucking amazing bod, and I have, for this occasion, I put aside my very best, lovely lovely blow, for Carol, who, no, I care about very deeply. So, okay, get to Shea, it's fucking *bat* night, everybody with the bats, fifty thousand bat-wielding sociopaths, security is very tight. I have a private booth. In the circle. This is through GE, my little addictive exec at GE. So we entree, me and Carol, and my client, I see, has fucked me over, 'cause there's already someone there, you know who, that talk-show guy, he's always got like three drag queens and a Satanist, and he's there with a girl can't be more than fourteen. "Oops." This fucking guy, my *daughter* watches that show. And between us, heavy substance abuser. I ask him to leave. I mean I come to watch a ball game with my good friend Carol and I'm forced to encounter skeevy baby-fucking cokeheads. One thing leads to the other, politeness out the window he comes at me Mets ashtray in his hand. What do I do. [KIM: You have a bat.] I have a bat, I take this bat, I acquaint this individual in the head with this bat. "Ba-doing." Right, ba-doing? He doesn't go down. Stands there, walks out the door, comes back two security guards. "Is there a problem here, boys?" "Well sir, this man, bicka bicka bicka," "Yes, I completely understand and here's something for your troubles." [KIM: How much?] How much, Kim? How much did I give these good men to resolve our altercation? I gave them one thousand dollars in U.S. currency. And they were very grateful. Mister Microphone sits down, doesn't speak, doesn't move rest of the night.

Moody fucking person. Mets take it, great ball, home with Carol where we romp in the flower of our youth. I win. I dominate. I get all the marbles. And that is why I love New York.

SEPARATION by Tom Kempinski

An aspiring New York actress with a degenerative bone disease strikes up a bizarre long-distance relationship with a playwright in London who is afraid to leave his apartment. Their conversations blossom into a hesitant and troubled romance, spanning two cities and two frightened people's hearts.

JOE, mid-to-late forties, English, learns that Sarah has a job in a new play.

SCENE: In Joe's apartment. On the phone.

TIME: The present.

JOE: (*JOE, in his own thoughts, gets up and walks to the edge of his room near hers.*) You do realize, you're on your way, you're crossed over into ordinary life, out of the handicapped life, I mean that's what this means… [SARAH: (*She senses from his not answering her that what she fears may be near.*) Well, I don't know, you'd have to say tha…] (*Going on*) I mean directors who see you in the play won't know you use crutches yourself, of course they'll find out when they offer you a job, but by then some will take you anyway, I mean this could lead to regular work, you know, just natural living… [SARAH: Oh come on, one rose doth not a summer make, right, the industry's not…] (*JOE's apparent excitement for her and his common-sense explanations now become increasingly filled and taken over by bitterness.*) No, no, but it does, that's what it means, it does, you'll be up and away getting work, going to auditions with your non-special friends, reminding directors of the success you had with "The Empty Palate," and the old, fat fart who set the whole thing in motion will soon be forgotten along with the heart-felt protestations of special feelings and all the rest of the fraudulent nonsense, of course; which is why you haven't been over to see me as soon as you got some tiny part in an eminently forgettable play, right?... [SARAH: (*SARAH has got up, frightened and horrified, and now stands near the side of her room next to Joe's—They are very close.*) Joe, I told you it's purely medical reasons which have kept...] (*He interrupts, sarcastic, but still holding back the final wave of rage.*) Oh come on, come on, happens all the time, people do your plays, they *love* the part, they *love* the play, they come over to tea for chats about the character, they reveal little bits of themselves to ingratiate themselves with you—the writer who gives them life—but actually they conceal everything; they pretend love, they conceal mere need. The play opens, it's a flop or a hit, down comes the shutter, you never see them again, and if you meet again by chance, you're strangers, ain't I right, are you saying it's not so?... [SARAH: (*Fear makes her voice a little shrill.*) I'm saying that with us it's different, with us it's very, very...] (*Forty-five years of bitterness and feelings of betrayal erupt out of JOE.*) Oh, please! Don't bleed all over me, O.K., we're not in the operating theatre now, you're going to bugger off like all the rest of them, you've had your pound of flesh, you've sucked the old carcass dry, so now the carrion crow moves on to corpses new, oh yes, true to form, my bird, true to type. You of course can act while I can't write, so I am left once again to sit on my slowly thinning arse and contemplate the wreck of my life and wonder why I persist and persist and persist in choosing faithless, phoney women who begin by showering me with their most ardent displays of affection and love and then throw me out like a dead dog over a cliff, *that,* doctor, is the little problem we must spend the *next* forty years or so looking into, don't you think, wouldn't you say so, eh, doc, hmm...(*Roars*) WELL WOULDN'T YOU SAY SO, SARAH!!!?...

SHOWBIZ RABBI (from the revue *Showing Off*) by Douglas Bernstein and Denis Markell

---

Meet an unusual RABBI, in his late twenties or thirties.

SCENE: Los Angeles Synagogue.

TIME: The present.

(*Sounds of religious chanting from off-stage*)

(*Lights up on a RABBI wearing a jogging outfit and an L.A. Dodger hat*)

Thank you. Thank you very much, Cantor Segal. Ladies and Gentlemen! (*He leads the applause*) Thank you, Cantor. Always gets the holidays off on the right note, doesn't he?

So...welcome. For those of you who are new to the Temple of the Performing Arts here in Los Angeles, or don't attend our regular bi-monthly Sabbath services, I am Rabbi Dave—David Stone. And I am just thrilled to be back for another High Holiday season. Rosh Hashanah and Yom Kippur, or as my Writers Guild friends like to call them—"The Big Blast" and "The Big Fast"...I'm kidding. We've got a really great service planned for you tonight and tomorrow; it's gonna be (*à la Ed Sullivan*) a really big show.

And speaking of show—how many people saw *Sho-ah* on the Z channel the other night? (*He asks for hands*) Did you see it? (*Shakes his head*) It was something. I did a special on the film when it first came out on *The Rabbi Dave Hour*—seen every Thursday night at 10 on Cable channel K.

But enough of the Holocaust—let's get started with Erev Rosh Hashanah! Maestro, if you please!

(*The organ plays something appropriate while the Rabbi moves to the podium*)

How 'bout our organist?—Mr. Marvin Hamlisch? (*Applause*) Marvin, play a little bit of that one I love.

(*Marvin plays a bit of "The Sting"*)

He wrote that, he tells me. Now let's begin the service.

[(*A voice: "The service will begin on page five."*)]

Thank you, Sy. I guess you all remember Sy, who has been for so many years, the Voice of Password. Welcome back, Sy.

[SY: (*V.O.*) Thank you, Rabbi.]

I know we all want to say thanks to Mr. and Mrs. Shecky Greene for our new prayer books. Every year we have a problem with the prayer books, but I think we've solved it this year—we're using *The Rabbi Dave High Holiday Prayerbook*, edited by Rabbi David Stone. I

113

thought why not. I sort of mixed and matched my favorite parts of all the services. There are some puzzles in there for the kids...and some delicious recipes for the ladies—by my lovely wife, Barbara. (*He looks at "Barbara"*) Thank you, Darling.

[SY: The service will begin on page five.]

(*Starts, looks up*) Yes, Barbara? Oh, I almost forgot—I'll be calling on the esteemed members of our congregation here at the Temple for the Performing Arts to help us today. Mr. Red Buttons will do the Hamotzi. My good good friend Mr. Stevie Spielberg on Kiddush. Special Guest Cantor Steve Lawrence is here to lead the Sh'ma with, of course, Special Guest Cant-tress Eydie Gorme. And our Torah service is terrific, I don't care who they got at Rodoph Shalom—our Aliyahs are gonna kill. Listen to this line-up: Mr. Sandy Koufax (*He points to his cap*), Mr. Jack Klugman (*Pianist plays "Odd Couple" theme*), Mr. Monty Hall—choosing Torah number one, Torah number two, or Torah number three. And our last Aliyah, our Maftir, this evening...Mr. Uri Geller! Uri Geller! So the torahs are gonna be bending and flying all over the place...you're gonna want to stick around for that, I am sure.

Now, what'd I forget? (*Looks at Barbara*) Ah, right! As you know, the Japanese have purchased this mall—so Temple for the Performing Arts will once again be on location for next year's high holidays.

We spoke to the Hollywood Bowl, and they're okay on Rosh Hashanah—but they've got the Simon Wiesenthal Ice Show on Yom Kippur. But our people are talking to Simon's people and I'm sure we'll work it out.

In any event, please use our Yom Kippur 800 number—and Atone-By-Phone. Okay...(*He opens his prayer book, and flips the pages*) Boruch...Ata...I dunno...

[SY: Dave?]

Yes, Sy?

[Voice: Fourth inning. Dodgers 5, Orioles 3.]

Sy will be keeping us posted on the World Series score all throughout the service. Now let's begin...(*Pianist starts to play "What I Did For Love"*)

Wait! Oh, I don't believe it. That's all the time we have, Ladies and Gentlemen. Happy New Year, everybody! L'Shana Haba-aw

B'Yerushalayim. Next year in Jerusalem. Or maybe I should say—
L'Shana Haba-aw Belair! Goodnight, folks!!
   (*Organ music up as lights fade*)

SIGHT UNSEEN by Donald Margulies

JONATHAN WAXMAN, a famous American-Jewish painter in his thirties, comes to England for his first major London show. He visits his former girlfriend, Patricia, whom he hasn't seen in fifteen years. During their reminiscences, Jonathan reflects on his father who has recently died.

SCENE: Patricia and her husband's English farmhouse.

TIME: The present.

   JONATHAN: My father, God!, my father *loved* seeing my name in print. *My* name, after all, was *his* last name. Got such a kick out of it. Eight pages in the Sunday Times. He couldn't believe *The New York Times* could possibly have that much to say about *his* kid. "All these words," he said, "are about *you*? What is there to say about *you*?" He was serious; he wasn't just teasing. Oh, he was teasing, too, but it threatened him. No, it did. It pointed up the fact that he could be my father and still not know a thing about me. Not have a clue. What did the fancy-schmancy art world see that he didn't? What were those big dirty paintings about, anyway? So then when all the hype started...that's very seductive in the beginning, I got to admit. Vindicating, even: "Ah ha! See? I *am* a genius. *Now* maybe my father will respect me." But it had the opposite effect on him. It didn't make him proud. It bewildered him. It alienated him. How could *he* have produced a "visionary"? It shamed him somehow. I can't explain. (*A beat.*) I went to pack up his house the other day? My parents' house? All his clothes, my old room, my mother's sewing machine, all those rooms of furniture. Strange being in a place where no one lives anymore. Anyway, what I found was, he'd taken all the family pictures, everything that was in albums, shoved in drawers—hundreds of them—and covered an entire wall with them, floor to ceiling, side to side. I first saw it years ago, when he'd started. It was his Sistine

115

Chapel; it took him years. He took my hand (I'll never forget this) he took my hand—he was beaming: "*You're* an artist," he said to me, "*you'll* appreciate this." He was so proud of himself I thought I was gonna cry. Proud and also in a strange way competitive? So, there was this wall. The Waxman family through the ages. Black-and-white, sepia, Kodachrome. My great-grandparents in the shtetl, my brother's baby pictures on top of my parents' courtship, me at my bar mitzvah. Well, it was kind of breathtaking. I mean, the sweep of it, it really was kind of beautiful. I came closer to examine it—I wanted to see how he'd gotten them all up there—and then I saw the staples. Staples! Tearing through the faces and the bodies. "Look what you've done," I wanted to say, "How could you be so thoughtless? You've ruined everything!" But of course I didn't say that. How could I? He was like a little boy. Beaming. Instead I said, "Dad! What a wonderful job!" (*A beat.*) So, there I was alone in his house, pulling staples out of our family photos. These documents that showed where I came from. Did they mean anything to him at all? I mean as artifacts, as proof of a former civilization, when my mother was vibrant and he was young and strong and we were a family? (*A beat.*) That's all gone now. It's all gone.

SIGHT UNSEEN by Donald Margulies·

JONATHAN WAXMAN, a famous American-Jewish painter in his thirties, comes to England for his first major London show there. Jonathan, in a press interview, talks about what art means to people nowadays and touches on the nature of fame and success to the artist.

JONATHAN: I remember, years ago, the big van Gogh show at the Met? The place was packed. Like Yankee Stadium. Buses emptied out from all over; Jersey, Westchester. All kinds of people. The masses. Average middle-class people. Like they were coming into the city for a matinee and lunch at Mamma Leone's. Only this was Art. Art with a capital A had come to the shopping mall generation and Vincent was the chosen icon. Now, I have nothing against van Gogh. Better him than people lining up to see the kids with the big eyes. But as I braved that exhibit—and it was rough going, believe me—I couldn't help but think of Kirk Douglas. Kirk Douglas should've gotten a cut of the house.

See, there's this Hollywood packaging of the artist that gets me. The packaging of the mystique. Poor, tragic Vincent: he cut off his ear 'cause he was so misunderstood but still he painted all these pretty pictures. So ten bodies deep they lined up in front of the paintings. More out of solidarity for Vincent (or Kirk) than out of any kind of love or passion for "good art." Hell, some art lovers were in such a hurry to get to the postcards and prints and souvenir placemats, they strode past the paintings and skipped the show entirely! Who can blame them? You couldn't *experience* the paintings anyway, not like that. You couldn't *see anything*. The art was just a backdrop for the *real* show that was happening. In the gift shop!

Now, you got to admit there's something really strange about all this, this kind of *frenzy* for art. I mean, what *is* this thing called art? What's it for? What does it do? Why have people historically drunk themselves to death over the creation of it, or been thrown in jail, or whatever? I mean, how does it serve the masses? *Can* it serve the—I ask myself these questions all the time. Every painting I do is another attempt to come up with some answers. The people who crowded the Met to look at sunflowers, I mean, why *did* they? 'Cause they *thought* they should. 'Cause they thought they were somehow enriching their lives. Why? *'Cause the media told them so!*

What *am* I today? I'm new here. I just got here. People like you suddenly care what I have to say.

It cracks me up that you do; it amuses me. You know, up till like eight or nine years ago, let's not forget, I was painting *apart*ments for a living. Apartments. Walls. Rooms. I was good at it, too. I didn't make a lot of money, but I didn't *need* a lot of money. I'd lose myself all day while I painted moldings, then I'd go home and do my *own* painting all night. A good, simple, hard-working life.

Then, like I said, like nine years ago, my world started getting bigger. I couldn't even retrace the steps; I can't remember how it happened. All I know is I met certain people and got a gallery and a show and the public started to discover my work. The night of my first opening, it's like these strangers witnessed a birth, like the work had no life before they laid eyes on it. We know that's ridiculous, of course, but this is what happens when you take your art out of your little room and present it to the public: it's not yours anymore, it's *theirs,* theirs to see with their own eyes. And, for each person who sees your work for the first time, you're discovered all over again. That begins to take its toll. You can't be everybody's discovery. That gets to be very demanding. Who *are* these people who are suddenly throwing money at you and telling you how wonderful and talented you are? What do *they* know? You begin to believe them. They begin to want things from you. They begin to expect things. The work loses its importance, the importance becomes "Waxman."

SIX DEGREES OF SEPARATION by John Guare

PAUL, a black man in his early twenties, has conned his way into the posh New York apartment of an art dealer and his wife, Ouisa and Flan. They are examples of the politically correct and the socially concerned; he is an example of a con man par excellence, who has convinced them he is the son of Sidney Poitier, knows their children, and graduated from Harvard. They inquire about his thesis and how he became intrigued with its subject.

TIME: The present.

PAUL: Well...

A substitute teacher out on Long Island was dropped from his job for fighting with a student. A few weeks later, the teacher returned to the classroom, shot the student unsuccessfully, held the class hostage and then shot himself. Successfully. This fact caught my eye: last sentence. *Times.* A neighbor described him as a nice boy. Always reading *Catcher in the Rye.*

The nitwit—Chapman—who shot John Lennon said he did it because he wanted to draw the attention of the world to *The Catcher in the Rye* and the reading of that book would be his defense.

And young Hinckley, the whiz kid who shot Reagan and his press secretary, said if you want my defense all you have to do is read *Catcher in the Rye.* It seemed to be time to read it again.

[FLAN: I haven't read it in years. (LOUISA *shushes* FLAN.)]

I borrowed a copy from a young friend of mine because I wanted to see what she had underlined and I read this book to find out why this touching, beautiful, sensitive story published in July 1951 had turned into this manifesto of hate.

I started reading. It's exactly as I remembered. Everybody's a phoney. Page two: "My brother's in Hollywood being a prostitute." Page three: "What a phony slob his father was." Page nine: "People never notice anything."

Then on page twenty-two my hair stood up. Remember Holden Caulfield—the definitive sensitive youth—wearing his red hunter's cap. "A deer hunter hat? Like hell it is. I sort of closed one eye like I was taking aim at it. This is a people-shooting hat. I shoot people in this hat."

Hmmm, I said. This book is preparing people for bigger moments in their lives than I ever dreamed of. Then on page eighty-nine: "I'd rather push a guy out the window or chop his head off with an ax than sock him in the jaw...I hate fist fights...what scares me most is the other guy's face..."

I finished the book. It's a touching story, comic because the boy wants to do so much and can't do anything. Hates all phoniness and only lies to others. Wants everyone to like him, is only hateful, and is completely self-involved. In other words, a pretty accurate picture of a male adolescent. And what alarms me about the book—not the book so much as the aura about it—is this: The book is primarily about paralysis. The boy can't function. And at the end, before he can run away and start a new life, it starts to rain and he folds.

Now there's nothing wrong in writing about emotional and intellectual paralysis. It may indeed, thanks to Chekhov and Samuel Beckett, be the great modern theme.

The extraordinary last lines of *Waiting For Godot*—"Let's go." "Yes, let's go." Stage directions: They do not move.

But the aura around this book of Salinger's—which perhaps should be read by everyone *but* young men—is this: It mirrors like a fun house mirror and amplifies like a distorted speaker one of the great tragedies of our times—the death of the imagination.

Because what else is paralysis?

The imagination has been so debased that imagination—being

imaginative—rather than being the lynchpin of our existence now stands as a synonym for something outside ourselves like science fiction or some new use for tangerine slices on raw pork chops—what an imaginative summer recipe—and *Star Wars*! So imaginative! And *Star Trek*—so imaginative! And *Lord of the Rings*—all those dwarves—so *imaginative*—

The imagination has moved out of the realm of being our link, our most personal link, with our inner lives and the world outside that world—this world we share. What is schizophrenia but a horrifying state where what's in here doesn't match up with what's out there?

Why has imagination become a synonym for style?

I believe that the imagination is the passport we create to take us into the real world.

I believe the imagination is another phrase for what is most uniquely *us.*

Jung says the greatest sin is to be unconscious.

Our boy Holden says "What scares me most is the other guy's face—it wouldn't be so bad if you could both be blindfolded—most of the time the faces we face are not the other guys' but our own faces. And it's the worst kind of yellowness to be so scared of yourself you put blindfolds on rather than deal with yourself..."

To face ourselves.

That's the hard thing.

The imagination.

That's God's gift to make the act of self-examination bearable.

SIX DEGREES OF SEPARATION by John Guare

Two teenagers, RICK and his girlfriend, Elizabeth, have moved from Utah to become actors in New York. They have met Paul, a sophisticated young con-artist who persuades Rick to withdraw two hundred fifty dollars from the bank, so he can go meet his father, who he claims will immediately pay them back.

Rick delivers this monologue a short time before commiting suicide.

SCENE: New York City.

RICK: (*to us*) He told me he had some of his own money and he wanted to treat me. We went to a store that rented tuxedos and we dressed to the nines. We went to the Rainbow Room. We danced. High over New York City. I swear. He stood up and held out my chair and we danced and there was a stir. Nothing like this ever happened in Utah. And we danced. And I'll tell you nothing like that must have ever happened at the Rainbow Room because we were asked to leave. I tell you. It was so funny.

And we walked out and walked home and I knew Elizabeth was waiting for me and I would have to explain about the money and calm her down because we'll get it back but I forgot because we took a carriage ride in the park and he asked me if he could fuck me and I had never done anything like that and he did and it was fantastic. It was the greatest night I ever had and before we got home he kissed me on the mouth and he vanished.

Later I realized he had no money of his own. He had spent my money—our money—on that night at the Rainbow Room.

How am I going to face Elizabeth? What have I done? What did I let him do to me? I wanted experience. I came here to have experience. But I didn't come here to do this or lose that or be this or do this to Elizabeth. I didn't come here to be *this*. My father said I was a fool and I can't have him be right. What have I done?

A SMALL FAMILY BUSINESS by Alan Ayckbourn

JACK McCRACKEN finds out that the world of business is a snap compared to the perfidy and treachery within his own family. Jack, in his forties, has just taken over the furniture business from his father-in-law, Ken. At a family celebration, he addresses his assembled family—all of whom are in the business—with a hopefulness, sincerity, and earnestness that will soon prove to be incredibly naive.

SCENE: A modern house in present-day England.

JACK: Thank you, Ken. I'll do my best. I'm bracing myself for the culture shock of jumping from fish fingers to furniture—and I hope you'll have observed that all the fixtures and fittings in this house have come from the right place. Well, a man's got enough problems without in-law trouble as well... [(*Laughter.*)] Well. I think we're all aware that the business hasn't been as healthy as it might have been, just lately. Demand is sluggish, we know that. Consequently, productivity's also down and generally, I think it's fair to say—so far as I can gather, everyone's lost a bit of heart. Now it's very hard in this country for a businessman to say something even halfway idealistic, without people falling over backwards laughing. To them it sounds like a contradiction in terms, anyway. But. Putting it as simply as I can. If I do nothing else, and during the coming months I can assure you I plan to do plenty, but if I succeed in doing nothing else I am determined to introduce one simple concept. And that concept is basic trust. (*He pauses for effect.*)

[KEN: Basic what did he say?

YVONNE: Trust.

KEN: Oh, basic trust. Yes.]

I'm talking about establishing the understanding that so far as every individual member of that firm is concerned, working there is no longer going to be purely a question of take, take, take...whether it's raw materials from the shop floor, an extra fifty quid on our car allowances, or paper clips from the office. We're there because we actually believe in what we're producing. Let's try and put across the idea that many of us believe in it so strongly that we are even anxious to put something back in. Effort. Hard work. Faith. Where do you think we'd be if we could do that? I'll tell you, we'd be top of the bloody league, that's where we'd be. We're a small family business. Even today, we're still essentially the same as we always were. There's no them and us about it. When it comes down to it, it's all us. That's all there is. Us. Ken and Des and Roy, there. All the lads we have working for us; all the girls in the office. They're practically family themselves, aren't they? It shouldn't be that difficult to achieve. All I'm saying is—let's start with the paper clips, shall we? Start with trust, that's all... (*Slight pause.*) Sorry.

SMOKE ON THE MOUNTAIN by Connie Ray, conceived by Alan Bailey

A Saturday Night Gospel Sing featuring the Sanders Family in their first appearance on the gospel circuit in five years.

PASTOR OGLETHORPE, in his twenties, welcomes the congregation.

SCENE: Mount Pleasant Baptist Chruch in the depressed factory town of Mount Pleasant, North Carolina.

TIME: 1938.

PASTOR OGLETHORPE: God scratches where the world itches. (*Pause.*) The Apostle Paul wrote to Timothy about folks afflicted with itching ears, and I believe... (*He must confess.*) I do not know where they got off to. I purely do not. I directed them down to the Eat'n'Run over an hour ago, and they simply have not come back. They've been here, you see their things. The Eat'n'Run is usually true to its name. But I'm confident they'll be here any minute, so I'll press on and take this opportunity to welcome each and every one of you to the first-ever Saturday Night Sing at Mount Pleasant Baptist Church. I recall Job 35:10—But none saith, Where is God my maker, who gives song in the night. Amen. A special greeting to all you folks from the Antioch, Free Will, and Fire-Baptized Holiness. The doors of Mount Pleasant swing on welcome hinges. And I am surprised and delighted to see Miss Maude and Miss Myrtle in the Amen Corner. These dear ladies had some strong reservations about guitars and fiddles in the church, but I see you've had a change of heart. (*They haven't.*) I have not been this excited since I received the conviction to preach. I think it's a true sign of the modern times when we can gather together on a Saturday night, and I can look out on all the menfolk and see nothing but shirtsleeves! Not a suit coat in sight. When I received the call to this church after Preacher Dryman passed away—Does it seem like a year already?—I said to myself, Mervin, what can you bring the good folks at Mount Pleasant? (*PASTOR OGLETHORPE strolls away from the pulpit.*) And I studied on it, and the answer was progress. Here we are just two years shy of 1940, and look what God has wrought! Every time I look up at that electrical light bulb, I thank God—and the generous contributions of Miss Maude and Miss Myrtle—for progress. Us Baptists are pushing on into the modern world. You all look so good sitting out there, I think I'll take the liberty myself. It's hot.

SMOKE ON THE MOUNTAIN by Connie Ray, conceived by Alan Bailey

A Saturday Night Gospel Sing featuring the Sanders Family in their first appearance on the gospel circuit in five years.

BURL SANDERS, in his forties and leader of the Sanders clan, has been running a gas station. He describes building a present for his wife, Vera.

SCENE: Mount Pleasant Baptist Church in the depressed factory town of Mount Pleasant, North Carolina.

TIME: 1938.

BURL: And one day, I said, Vera, if President Roosevelt can borrow all that money for his WPA, CCC, FWA, and every other initial up there in Washington, I reckon I can borrow a parcel for your back porch. I loved building that porch. Ten by twenty feet, six posts—[VERA: Turned, not square.] Tongue and groove floor. I never feel closer to the Almighty than when I'm building something. I guess because Jesus was a carpenter himself. [THE SANDERS FAMILY and PASTOR OGLETHORPE: Amen.] But about halfway through that porch, something happened. My business at the station just dried up. I'm telling you, nobody stopped. I was sitting in front of the store one day and a DeSoto I know WELL flew by so fast, I couldn't get my hand up to wave… [VERA: (*Bursting with it.*) It takes very little investigation on my part to find out the store up the road is selling beer!] (*Shaken by his wife's interruption.*) Selling beer on Highway 11. Overnight it was a real popular establishment. [VERA: Wine is a mocker and beer a brawler; whoever is led astray by them is not wise. Proverbs 20:1.] (*Interrupting.*) Thank you, Mother. [VERA: (*Sliding back into the pew.*) You're welcome.]

Now, it's always been my conviction to sell only what the Lord would eat and drink. But I'm sitting there with a half-built porch, a loan due at the bank, a family of five, (*To STANLEY*) six to feed, and I have not sold so much as a cellophane cracker in three days. (*The reference to STANLEY sends a tense wave through the rest of the family. STANLEY does not like "having to be fed."*) And just like the icing on the cake, you-know-who drives up. Big old Mercury car, one of them pricey felt hats like they wear in town. He was...What's that word you use, Denise? Suave. And I thought to myself, as I'm watching him crawl out, this man reminds me of somebody. He takes hold of my hand and is shaking and grinning like I've been shook and grinned at so many times.

And this beer man sets right in to making his play. Oh, I'm gonna be a rich man to hear him tell it. Two cents on every bottle is mine to keep. [PASTOR OGLETHORPE: Two cents?] He's talking profits and revenues, and I'm seeing the bank take over my store, my family wasting to nothing. Now, I've never told this, not even to my family, but...I was backed into a corner here. I thought, "That's it. I'm gonna have to do it. I'm gonna have to sell beer in my store."

And just as I'm about to say load it in, the beer man's car starts hissing. Hissing and moaning out the back, a-rocking on its tires like there's something alive back there. Then Pow! Just like a rabbit gun going off. Pow. POW. The beer man's done hit the ground and crawled up under a bench. I am froze like a popsicle.

BOOM! That trunk lid blows open and a bottle cap flies by my head so close it just about pins my ear to the clapboard. Well, I am defrosted and down in the dirt with the beer man.

And it hit me. The Devil! [(*THE FAMILY murmurs agreement.*) VERA: The Devil.] This here beer man reminds me of old Satan himself. And I could be Job, only in the modern world. And I thought on Job. Now, there he was, robbed of every sign of God's favor, hunkered down in a sack, covered with festering sores and boils, and the miracle is, he NEVER lost faith. And here I am, put to the test one time, and I'm ready to roll over.

Well, I strode over to that bench, I jerked that beer man up by his fancy lapels, I put my nose right up to his, and I said, "Bud, I suggest you crawl back in that stinking Mercury and haul it down the road." He jumps in the front seat a-sputtering and crying and takes off, beer dripping down through the cracks and dribbling on the tires. Shoo-ee.

Now, for those of you who don't know it, that beer has staying power. [(*The rest of THE FAMILY agrees. BURL moves up to STANLEY and gets his guitar.*)] I got the family down there. We set in to scrubbing and shoveling dirt onto the puddles of it. Psalms 62:8 says—Mother? [VERA: (*Caught off guard.*) Trust in Him at all times.] Trust in Him at all times. I won't sell beer in my store. And I don't do near as well as I did. I finished the porch, though. (*To FAMILY.*) We're just going to have to wait a while for the screen wire. [THE SANDERS FAMILY: Yes, sir.] (*BURL starts playing the introduction to "The Filling Station." THE FAMILY moves into position.*)

(*Trying to drum up a little business.*) That bottle cap's still stuck in the siding. Next time you're up on Highway 11, pull in—I'll show it to you.

SPIELE '36 by Steve Carter

Because of Hitler's displeasure and political machinations of American officials, the Jewish athletes are forbidden to run in the Berlin 1936 Olympics.

The black runners on the team decide to boycott the race to show solidarity with their Jewish teammates. But one of them, OLIVER, eighteen, refuses and explains to another, Gus, why.

SCENE: The room of two Jewish runners, Herman and Lux, in Berlin.

TIME: 1936.

OLIVER: No! I'm running! I know what we agreed, Gus, but I have to renege. I don't have words like you, but I know I have to run this race. Every night, I've been having this dream. I dream about Joe Louis being beaten to a pulp by Schmeling. The night it happened, my whole family just sat there...crying. Everybody in the neighborhood just cried. The next day, nobody who was colored could raise their head. We couldn't look one another in the eye. We were…lost. We had all been knocked out too. Well, I dream about it almost every night and I see Adolf Hiltler's face…laughing and spitting at Joe while he's crumpled up there. I always knew that I was going to win three medals because I'm just that good. But in my heart, I've been asking myself, especially these last two months, what I could do to make the world sit up and get back at Adolf Hitler and Max Schmeling. I'm going to run and get four medals. I want to avenge Joe Louis and let Hilter and Schmeling see my ass in their faces. Those are your words, Gus. Guess I don't have any of my own, but I figure if these people can put out leaflets and things and say, openly, that they want to get rid of Lux and Herman, here…what will they do to you and me after they're through with them?

SQUARE ONE by Steve Tesich

Dianne and ADAM, a couple in their thirties, meet in a dystopian country in the future where everyone lives cooperatively and all feelings, art, and individuality have been co-opted by the state.

Dianne and Adam have a baby but they lose it. Here, Adam watches with Dianne as the baby dies.

SCENE: Their apartment, filled with stuffed animals.

TIME: The future.

ADAM: You've read the literature. All we can do is let nature take its course. [DIANNE *cries out.*] You mustn't torture yourself like that. It does no good. You don't have to prove anything to me. I know exactly how you feel, because I feel the same way. Just because we don't flaunt our agony the way they used to doesn't mean it's not there. Our humanity's our own affair. We don't have to prove it to anybody.
   (*The baby's cry rises a bit. Subsides.*)
   At least…
   (*It rises again. He waits for it to subside.*)

127

At least, if nothing else, this poor little thing can give voice to its torment. Whereas I, we, we have to bear ours in silence. And how much harder that is. How much more persuasive. And you mustn't forget...

(*The crying rises again. He waits for it to subside. It doesn't. He raises his voice to ride over it.*)

You mustn't ever forget that we don't really know for sure that the poor little thing is in any pain at all. You've read the literature, the journals, the brochures, the copyrighted stories. Written by authorities on the subject of suffering and pain. And all of them concur that in cases such as this, there is no suffering to speak of. As a matter of fact...

(*The baby's crying subsides and so does his voice.*)

As a matter of fact, they suspect just the opposite. They suspect that in cases such as this there is a state of acceptance. A state of numbness that's not really a numbness but a kind of peace. But no suffering to speak of. I know, I realize, to you, to me, to us, to any layman what we're hearing now sounds very much like suffering but that's because we've been conditioned to interpret it in a certain way, whereas the truth, according to all the data on hand, points in just the opposite direction.

[DIANNE: I know. I've read the literature.

ADAM: Not all the literature.

DIANNE: No, not all.

(*It cries very weakly now.*)

My poor little baby. What can I do?]

If you had read all the literature, the periodicals, the weeklies, the monthlies, the quarterlies, you would know that there is nothing you can do. Not in cases such as this. Actually, they warn against trying. Nine times out of ten, and here I'm quoting, nine times out of ten, you can do more harm than good.

(*The crying is fading.*)

[DIANNE: It's looking at me. Such large eyes for one so small.]

If it's any comfort to you it really can't see you. In cases such as this, the eyes stay open, but they see nothing anymore. It's all peaceful and dark.

STAND UP TRAGEDY by Bill Cain

LEE, a fourteen year old boy, gifted in drawing, dreams of going to art school. He lives with a sister, Maritza, whom his alcoholic mother abuses, and his brother, Tyro, who steals. Here, he reenacts three days in his home, while students, who include Marco and Henry and Carlos, provide a chorus. Saga is a comic book hero-knight Lee has created to mirror his own ambitions to fly away but who, like him, is earthbound.

SCENE: In and around a small Catholic School for Hispanic boys on the lower east side of Manhattan.

TIME: The present.

(*LEE will now go through three nights and days with his family in the apartment. The rest of the cast will provide the sounds of the apartment and the streets.*)

LEE: I don't belong here.

What do you mean you don't belong here? This is your home.

I don't even have a bed here.

I'm sleeping with Maritza now. Lee. You got a problem with that?

You can sleep on the couch.

Why do you want me here?

You spend the night on the streets?

Yes.

Oh, no. Oh, no. You're not going to be running the streets like your brother having the police bring you home cause the police, they've been through this apartment too many times for your brother.

So throw Tyro out.

You see? You see who's starting it. Is it him or me?

Tyro, where's my walkman?

I don't know. I didn't touch it.

Tyro, where is it?

He said he didn't touch it.

At least give me some of the money from it.

You saying I stole it?

Just give me some of the money. I don't care what you did with it.

129

I didn't steal it.

And you rob me. You think I don't know where the money goes out of my purse? Lee, now I have to sleep with my money in my hands at night. Someday I'm going to call the police on *you*, then you see how you like it.

[STUDENTS: Slap.

TEACHERS: Slap *back*.

STUDENTS: Hit.

TEACHERS: Kick kick kick.

STUDENTS: Knock down.]

Like a dance. I wonder if it's going to be hard to get back into the dance?

Lee! Lee! Lee! Help me!

Into the dance I go. Slam. Slam. Slam Dance.

[STUDENTS: SA-GA! SA-GA! SA-GA!]

NO! NO! I WILL NOT DISAPPEAR INTO SAGA! FIGHT—KICK—BLEED—ACHE—BUT I WON'T BE SAGA. I WON'T TRY TO ESCAPE.

(Night.)

They sleep. Let them sleep. I won't shut my eyes. I will draw. I will do my portfolio. But not what I see.

No, I will dream. I will imagine impossible things. I will pretend I can see fruit. Fruit on a table.

With a table cloth and a candle. I will pretend that fruit is real. Oranges. I will draw bottles.

And I will pretend that I don't see them turning into animals in the night making animal noises while they do animal things while the children are hiding under the bed.

Fruit. Tables.

I will make up trees.

I will imagine morning.

(Morning)

I could of been an artist too. I could of gone to Art and Design.

I'm not in it yet.

Hey, these aren't bad, Lee. I mean they look like things. Fruit. Lots of fruit. What, all you draw now is fruit?

Why don't you draw Saga again, Lee?

130

[ALL: SAGA! SA-GA! SA-GA!]

NO. NO SAGA. I will see what's here. I will not change it. I will let it be what it is.

(Evening)

LEE! LEE! LEE! Get your brother off me! *LEE! HELP!*

I am ice. I will not move. I am freezing. I can't feel my feet.

LEE! Jesus Christ, Lee, is that what they teach you in that school? Not to help your mother?

You're his mother too. *Leave her alone!*

YOU FIGHT HER BECAUSE SHE'S THE ONLY ONE YOU CAN BEAT!

THEY LAUGH AT YOU ON THE STREET.

YOU TAKE DRUGS SO YOU DON'T HAVE TO HEAR THEM LAUGHING.

[ALL: Slap. Hit. Hit.]

YOU BUY GUNS BECAUSE YOU THINK MARITZA DOESN'T LIKE IT WHEN YOU DO IT TO HER!

[ALL: SLAP. HIT. SLAP. HIT. HIT. HIT.]

COME ON AND HIT ME HARDER BECAUSE I DON'T WANT TO SAY THESE THINGS. *KNOCK ME OUT* BECAUSE I DON'T WANT TO KNOW THESE THINGS. YOU ARE *ALWAYS* GOING TO BE MY BROTHER! YOU ARE *ALWAYS* GOING TO BE MY MOTHER!

[ALL: SAGA! SAGA! SAGA!

CARLOS: I TELL YOU WHAT BOY AND WHAT IS TRUE BOY

YOU DIDN'T WANT ME—NOW I DON'T WANT YOU, BOY.

MARCO: YOU'RE NOT WORTHY OF CALLING MY NAME.

YOU'RE ON YOUR OWN BUT YOU KNOW THE REAL SHAME?

HENRY: YOU'RE ON YOUR OWN, YOU'RE FINALLY ALONE

AND IT'S BAD TO BE ALONE, BOY,

ALL: ALONE IN YOUR HOME.]

(Night)

We lie in bed and it's nice and it's sick and it's warm and the kids

131

climb out from under the bed and on top of us and they sleep and she says:

Lee, if you run away, take me with you.

And I think, if you're still with me, I haven't run away at all.

And they all whisper, "Take me with you, take me with you, with you, with you."

But I won't sleep. Move. No sleep. I've slept before. I have to see it all. I get my portfolio from where I hid it and I draw. I will do what Mr. Griffin says.

When they sleep they are all one animal with many souls. No, I don't draw that. My mother is a graceful curve. She is my child and the children are old. No, don't draw that.

Oranges: Apples. Apples. Apples.

(The next evening)

[KENTER: It's Christmas and our doors will be open until 11 p.m. every…

BRENNAN: It's 37 degrees in mid-town. Manhattan could be looking at some wet snow flurries…

LARKIN (singing, joined by all): Feliz Navidad, Feliz Navidad, Feliz Navidad.

ALL (singing): We wish you a Merry Christmas. We wish you…]

Dance! Come on. It's Christmas! Dance with me! Maritza's dancing. Dance! Dance! Dance!

Oh God, you're funny when you dance, Lee.

My first husband—he works at the bottle company down on Pitt by the bridge—shortest, baldest man in the world, but could he dance! Lee would have got his dancing from him, but he's not Lee's father so he must have got it from me. Lee! Lee! Lee dances good!

Get the fuck away from her.

Oh, so this is how it's going to start.

Come on, Tyro. Dance with me.

No, I'm not going to dance with you. You like to dance with Lee. Dance with Lee then.

I don't want to dance at all if that's the way you're going to be. I'm going.

You go when I say you go.

You don't own me.

Come on, kids, it's Christmas night.

You shut up. This is between me and her.

COME ON, LEE. YOU DANCED BEFORE. YOU DANCE NOW!

[ALL: Step. Slap. Hit. Hit.]

LEE: YOU WANT TO DANCE! DANCE WITH ME! COME ON, LEE! YOU WANT TO DANCE, BOY! DANCE WITH ME!!!

And you are always going to be my mother and you are always going to be my brother and I will NOT move. I will NOT MOVE. I MUST NOT MOVE. FREEZE! FREEZE! FREEZE!

Suddenly it's perfectly quiet. Am I dead?

They have stopped. They are looking at me. They can't go on.

Why?

WHY!?!

If it goes any further he kills her.

Well, good. *KILL HER! GET WHAT YOU WANT! I'M NOT GOING TO STOP YOU ANYMORE!*

I don't stop it but it stops—by itself.

The only way it can go on is if I try to stop it.

They don't want it over. He kills her and the checks stop coming and it's over. She throws him out and nobody touches her. *OH, JESUS! THEY WANT IT TO GO ON!*

And they look at one another like they don't know what to do.

They're embarrassed.

And she starts crying like I broke her heart because I won't save her from the fight.

WHAT FIGHT, Momi?

IT'S OVER.

THE FIGHT IS OVER!

THE SUBSTANCE OF FIRE by Jon Robin Baitz

Isaac Geldhart, a publisher of unfashionable books about the Holocaust, is at odds with his son Aaron, the company's fiscal expert, who wants to publish a more fashionable novel of dubious literary worth. This has led to a proxy fight in which Aaron's sister, an actress on children's TV, and brother, MARTIN, have to participate.

Martin, in his twenties, teaches landscape architecture at Vassar. Isaac has just accused Martin of having thoughts that are "poison."

SCENE: A conference room of the publishing house.

TIME: 1987.

MARTIN: Poison! You want to talk about poison? Look at what you've done. You've created a family of literary zombies. You know that people are afraid of you. It's why you've gotten so far. Yes. "Isaac Geldhart knows something, he came from some awful childhood in Europe that nobody knows about." He has a "seer-like standing in the book world." Blah-Blah-Blah—phooey. Let me tell you, we're fucked up by it. I grew up running around this building. When I was eight, you gave me the Iliad in Greek so that someday I could read it. Monster! People's lives are ruined by books and they're all you know how to relate to, Dad. You too, Aaron, for all your talk. You too, Sarah, pretending you hate to read. Sometimes I want to take a pruning shears and do an Oedipus on myself. I counted my books last week. Do you know how many I have? Want to take a guess? (*No one says anything.*) Fourteen thousand, three hundred, and eighty-six. The sixty crates of books that Mom left me. Well, I finally had them carted up the Hudson, but I had to have shelves built. The whole house. Every room. And instead of just guessing—I was, I mean— speechless. A wreck of a life. It just flashed before my eyes. No sex, no people, just books 'til I die. Dickens. In *French*. The bastard didn't write in French. What the fuck am I doing with *Dombey and Son* in French? The twelve-volume *Conquest of Mexico*. Two hundred cookbooks. The "Oxford World Classics," the little ones with the blue bindings, you know?

[Isaac: You got that?]

They're all just words. And this is life, and besides, I hear the book chains are now selling pre-emptive strike video games, so why bother anyway? I'm out.

134

THE SUM OF US by David Stevens

JEFF, a shy Australian in his twenties, lives with his Dad and works as a plumber. His mother died many years before.

In speculating about his homosexuality, Jeff points out to Dad that his grandmother—Dad's mom—was, in fact, a lesbian.

SCENE: Jeff and his Dad's sitting room in Footscray, Australia.

TIME: The present.

JEFF (*Turns to the audience.*): 'Strue. Granma was a dike. Well—a lesbian. She was a wonderful woman, though. I used to go down there for me holidays, and they were the best times. Wasn't anything flash, where she lived, a little weather board on the outskirts of town, where nothing worked right, and the plumbing looked like it was designed by Picasso. Obsessed with plumbing, Gran was. Maybe that's where I got the idea for going into the trade myself. And clean? Gran was always polishing every bit of woodwork in the house, you'd get up in the morning, and she'd be there, polishing away, so there was a lovely smell about the place, like lavender floor polish, cripes, I haven't seen that in the shops for yonks. Reminds of a funny story—but, well, that's a bit off, I s'ppose.

In the evenings we'd play Ludo, or Snakes and Ladders, or Tiddly Winks, I used to love those games with Gran. She used to keep an old Monopoly set hidden in the drawer, but Mary wouldn't let her play it, real strict, Salvation Mary was, and Gran too, but not as bad as Mary. Funny, int' it, someone as religious as Mary, going on about the devil and all his works, then jumping in the linen battlefield with Gran every night. Just goes to show, doesn't it? But I was staying there once, and Mary went out for the evening. Well, the minute Mary was out the door Gran whipped out the old Monopoly board and had it set up before you could say Ned Kelly, her eyes all glinting. Not a word to Mary, she said. I tell you, it was the best game of Monopoly I've ever played, like Gran and me were doing something really wrong, fire and brimstone stuff. Isn't it funny how ordinary mortal sin can be? First time I ever went to stay there, I was, oh, I dunno, six, maybe seven, and a couple of my cousins were there too, so I had to sleep on a spare bed in Gran and Mary's room.

And I remember, I can see it so clearly, waking up on the first morning I was there, it was still early, and looking across to Gran's big bed, an old brass bed it was, and there was Gran and Mary, tucked up in bed, wrapped up in each other's arms. Gran was snoring, I remember, and I lay in bed looking at them for, oh, ever such a long time, and it seemed—natural, somehow, I dunno. Like the most natural thing I'd ever seen. Like love.

She and Mary used to put the old uniform and bonnet on every Sunday morning, then they'd shove the roast in the oven and head off to the 11 a.m. at the Citadel. I'd have to go along too, coz Gran, she really believed it was the answer. So you'd join in the hymns, and shout out Salvation, and have a real good time. I remember once it was all going on, the band playing, and the Songstresses banging their tambourines, and everybody singing their little hearts out, and yelling Salvation, and it all got so exciting I went up and flung meself on the Mercy Seat. That got the old biddies clucking, I can tell you, just saved another soul for Jesus, everybody likes a bit of drama. I copped curry from Dad when he heard about it, coz he knew what had happened, he knew it didn't mean anything. I was only twelve. But they'd all wanted someone to do it and nobody was, so I did. I've always liked to do the right thing by people.

When we got back, the roast'd be ready, the little kitchen'd be all steamy and hot, with Gran banging on the taps to make 'em work, and making the gravy and carving the meat. Mary'd look after the veggies, that's all she ever did, she was a lazy cow. Boiled the life out of 'em for forty-five minutes. She never did like veggies and I think she was getting her own back on 'em. Afterwards Gran and Mary'd go upstairs to that big double bed, and do whatever they did. Pro'bly just slept, be too tired for anything else. You ever noticed that? When you're on with someone, well, it's always nice to play hide the one sausage, of course, but most of all, the nicest thing about going to bed with someone on a regular basis is when they just let you sleep. That's the bit I like, snuggled up all safe and sound in their arms. Not that I'm an expert on relationships, mind you, but it happened to me once, and it worked real nice. For a while. (*He doesn't want to remember that.*) I mean, you meet some blokes that treat sex like they're going twenty-seven rounds with Bruce Lee, but that wears me out. I don't see what it proves. Maybe that's why I've never had much luck in the romantic stakes. Maybe I haven't got a high enough sex drive. Maybe I'm a bit—ordinary. (*He glances at his father.*) Or maybe it's him, there's such a thing as being too well adjusted. There's been a couple of times blokes have stayed here, stayed the night, y'know, and then in the morning he comes in, they're fast asleep in me arms, he comes in, taps 'em on the shoulder, and says "Do you take sugar in yer tea?" It can be a bit unnerving, I suppose. So it could be him. More likely it's me. Maybe I am just a bit—dull.

THE SUM OF US by David Stevens

A prospective girlfriend asks DAD if he minds that his son is gay.

SCENE: The sitting room of a house in Footscray, Australia.

TIME: The present.

DAD: (*Looks at the audience.*) What can I possibly say? I've never been ashamed of Jeff, not ever. Disappointed, yes. Disappointed that he'll never find a girl and settle down. Disappointed that he'll never give me a grandson. Disappointed that my family's name will stop with him. And disappointed because I honestly think he's missing out on something—wonderful. I can't believe in my heart, that what my mother found with her girlfriend, or what Jeff might find with any bloke, is a patch on what I had with his mum. I believe it can be love, I know it can, I know Jeff's been in love, I watched him and I saw the pain, and I knew that it was love.

But what I had with his mum, the life we shared together, the rows and the good times, the struggles and the fun, and most of all, making him, making a baby, knowing I'd put the seed in there and watching it grow, and then seeing him—

I couldn't believe it—that we'd made this thing, his mum and me, this little, tiny, living thing, and I wanted to hold him in my arms forever, take him away somewhere, him and his mum, and keep them safe from the rest of the world. And watching him grow, and the relief when everything turned out all right, he could see and hear and talk, he wasn't retarded or disabled, and fretting about him when he was sick, and being angry with him when he was naughty, and teaching him, and dreaming dreams for him. That more than anything. The dreams of what he might become. I remember the first time he went to school, he didn't seem old enough, he didn't seem big enough to be setting out on such an adventure, but he was a cocky little shit, all set to take on the world. But the night before, I was tucking him into bed, and I kissed him, and he whispered to me, he said, is it going to be all right, Dad, at school, am I going to manage? It nearly broke my heart. And I remember so many things.

So yes, I'm disappointed that he won't ever experience those things, because I think they're important, I think they're what life is. But if he's never going to have those things then I want him to have all the things he can have. If he was a liar, or a thief, or a murderer, maybe that would be different, though I don't think so, he'd still be my son. But Jeff is a kind and generous man, and no one can deny that he is honest. Our children are only the sum of us, what we add up to. Us, and our parents, and our grandparents, and theirs and all the generations.

THE TALENTED TENTH by Richard Wesley

BERNARD's efforts to finance and own a black radio station lead him to look back at his past and figure out where he misplaced his idealism.

In his late thirties or early forties, Bernard has a wife, children, and a mistress. More and more, his life weighs him down. He remembers a time when life was more exciting and a girlfriend, Habiba, now dead, who inspired him.

SCENE: On top of a hill on the outskirts of a large northeastern city.

TIME: The present.

BERNARD: Yeah, let's see: I was a junior at Howard University.

Martin Luther King tried to lead a march across the Edmund Pettus Bridge in Selma, Alabama, but the local authorities had a law against it. Those were the days when there were laws down South against black people doing anything except being Negroes, if you get my drift. Well, Dr. King decided to march anyway and the local authorities attacked the marchers and threw them in jail. People all over the country called on President Johnson to do something. He seemed hesitant. Then Dr. King announced he would march again, this time all the way to the state capital, Montgomery. The Klan started making noises. Lyndon Johnson still hesitated, so the Student Nonviolent Coordinating Committee went into action. They had a local chapter not that far from campus. Habiba and I went down there right after philosophy class and signed up together. We were ready, y'all.

I remember my heart was beating a mile a minute. The both of us were so excited. We were finally in the big fight: Helping the Race in civil rights struggle. We were a real part of history. Damn!

The room was filled with nervous energy. People sang civil rights songs and hugged each other and held hands—men and women, black and white. I sat among them and listened to their talk. I even touched them when they weren't looking. Then came all of these speeches and pronouncements to get us fired up. Lots of clenched fists in the air. The room was hot and sweaty and filled with cigarette smoke. I felt a little dizzy and reached for Habiba. Someone started singing, "Precious Lord, Take My Hand" and people started joining in. We all held hands and closed our eyes and let the power of the song take hold of us. Then, Habiba started shaking and shivering and gasping for breath. She opened her eyes and looked at me. She said she had a race memory. She was with a group of runaway slaves. They were fleeing armed gunmen across a swamp. Then, they were trapped with no way out. They began to sing and the more they sang, the stronger they became. She saw the flash of gunfire. She felt the pain of the bullets. But they kept getting stronger. Then, Habiba screamed. Just like that. A scream like I'd never heard before. Everyone in the room just stopped. It was like we all felt what she felt. People began to moan and shout and chant. Bloods who had sworn off going to church and had sworn off the spirit possession of our parents and grandparents began to rock and shake and tremble—yeah, they got the Spirit that night!

All that college sophistication we had didn't mean a thing. The Spirit was calling us home, now! Habiba screamed again! Yes, sir! We were going down to the White House and we were gonna march all day and all night, as long as it took! 'Cause Dr. King needed us! The workers down in Mississippi needed us! Our people needed us! Yes, sir! We were gonna press on, that night! Ol' Lyndon Johnson, you better listen to us, man! 'Cause we comin'! Marching around your front lawn tonight, buddy! And you're gonna send those troops down to Selma and you're gonna sign that civil rights bill, too! Our time was at hand! This is the new young America talkin' and you better listen! Scream, Habiba! Scream, sister! Let us feel those bullets! Let us feel the lash! Scream! Don't let us forget! Bring us home, sister love! Bring us home! Yes, sir! Yes, sir! Teach! Teach!

(*Pause*)

We marched in shifts, twenty-four hours a day, seven days. Lyndon Johnson sent the troops and Dr. King made his pilgrimage to Montgomery where he gave one of the greatest speeches of his life. Still see that speech from time to time on TV. I was listening to it the other day when my oldest son came in and asked me if I could give him some money for new clothes. School was out and they were having a special holiday sale at the mall. Martin Luther King's birthday.

TALKING THINGS OVER WITH CHEKHOV by John Ford Noonan

JEREMY, early forties, has written a play about his past relationship with Marlene, an actress. When he runs into Marlene in the park, Jeremy gives her the play. When they meet again Jeremy explains how he survived the anxiety of waiting for her opinion. And about the collegial sympathy he received from an unexpected guest, the great nineteenth-century playwright, Anton Chekhov!

SCENE: On and around a bench in Central Park.

TIME: The present.

JEREMY: Thank God for Chekhov. He's the only one who can calm me down. After I left you yesterday, I stopped for one drink each at all these different bars. Only works me up more. Get home at 5, flip on *Six Million Dollar Man*. At 6 I switch to 11 for *The Jeffersons* and *Barney Miller*. At 7 back to 5 for *Mash*. I'm exploding. I throw on my sweats. Seventeen times around the block. Up my five flights three and four steps at a time. I swing open my door. Flop to the floor for a set of push-ups. I notice his foot. Stop. Look up. He's sitting in my favorite rocker. Beautiful white linen suit. Felt hat. Walking cane. In his hand a bottle of something Russian. "Like some kvass?" "What's kvass?" He smiles. Pours me half a glass. He toasts, "To you!" "Why me?" "Tomorrow you'll be hearing what people think of your first play." He continues. This visit he's speaking Russian but somehow I hear it in English. "Plays make your life no longer your own. With stories you write it, mail it, good-by. But plays! Rehearsals. Production meetings. Picking the actors." Suddenly he seems about to go on and on. More kvass. He laughs and says, "I don't mind my characters when they go on and on, but I hate to do it myself. How about more kvass?" Another half glass. Now I'm tipsy too. "Close Friend," he mumbles, "you and I are alike in a very big way. We're afraid to let go. We're both way too serious." I smile. He smiles. Now I know why he keeps coming back. He almost drops the bottle and chuckles, "From a tipsy Russian take some silly advice: ANY NUMBER OF PEOPLE CAN BE LUCKY ENOUGH TO WRITE ONE GOOD PLAY, BUT ONLY A FEW OF US ARE SMART ENOUGH TO DRESS LIKE WE'RE CAPABLE OF WRITING MANY!" Chekhov laughs. I laugh. No two writers have ever howled louder. He goes on, "It's not only how you dress. It's any little thing that makes business easier. The right pencils. Paper you love to touch. A chair to work in that makes your back never hurt. Your desk in front of a window you love to look out of." He grabs my hand so tight I yelp. "CLOSE FRIEND, CONCENTRATE ON THE LITTLE THINGS. THEY'RE THE ONLY THINGS THAT ADD UP." He gets up, flips open the door with his walking cane, and wobbles off.

TALKING THINGS OVER WITH CHEKHOV by John Ford Noonan

JEREMY, early forties, has written a play about his past relationship with Marlene, an actress.

Jeremy must rewrite his play but can't settle down to the task. Alcohol, cocaine, a little heroin, and a lot of prostitutes provide plenty of diversion. Finally, when he comes back home, none other than the great nineteenth-century playwright, Anton Chekhov, is there to give him advice.

SCENE: On and around a bench in Central Park.

TIME: The present.

JEREMY: I crawl up the stairs. Door open. He's nowhere to be seen. Suddenly I hear the toilet flush. The door opens. He's got on the smoking jacket Gorky gave him. He's wearing a smile I've never seen before. Already I'm pissed. "Waiting Friend," he says, "we'll need more toilet paper soon!" I want to rip out his throat. Next he directs me to the far wall. Where earlier he had scrawled, "GOOD ART NEVER EXCUSES BAD LIVING," now he's written, "LET ANTON CHEKHOV BE FOR YOU WHAT LEO TOLSTOY COULDN'T BE FOR HIM." He puts his arm around my shoulder. "Talented Friend," he says with just the trace of a French accent, "not only is dear Marlene right about the sex in Act II, but these two people can't end up together in the final scene." "Russian Schmuck," I scream, "it's why I'm doing it. To end up with her in the end!" [MARLENE: Jeremy, listen: if that's—] Suddenly Chekhov pulls out a copy of *Cherry Orchard.* "I had the same problem as you writing my final act. I wanted so badly for things to turn out happy. I was so desperate for Lopahin and Varya to end up together that I pulled my own ten-day vodka bender." Through his tears he talks on. "Like you, all I needed was someone looking over my shoulder. I went to Tolstoy. Much as the bouncing carriage hurts, I make his house in less than a day. I knock...The minute I see the white beard, I say, 'Uncle T, I am having trouble finishing the last act of my new play. Will you come and cast a warm shadow?' He laughs that laugh of his. 'Anton, your fiction is superb, but as I told you at the opening of *Three Sisters,* that snowy night in St. Petersburg, I hate your plays.' 'Uncle T, you were drunk.' 'I will tell you the same thing sober. YOU ARE WORSE THAN SHAKESPEARE, do you hear me, WORSE THAN SHAKESPEARE!' He slams the door. I begin to laugh. I crack the reigns. The sled starts for home. I keep laughing and yelling proudly at the snowy countryside, 'WORSE THAN SHAKESPEARE! WORSE THAN SHAKESPEARE.'" Marlene, I have never seen him so happy as he was in telling this story. That's when he turns to me, his smile fading as quickly as it had come. His hand lies heavy on my arm, the tears are filling up again, and in a choking, quavering whisper he says, "I had to let my characters not end up together, and you must do the same." That's when I pick him up and throw him down the stairs.

THOSE THE RIVER KEEPS by David Rabe

PHIL, in his thirties, an ex-con from Mulberry Street, is approached by Sal, an old friend from the east, to kill a man deeply in debt to the mob. Sal gets offended when Phil refuses, but Phil holds his ground: he's out of the life for good. Phil is already upset with himself for having killed a friend's dog since his release. Sal, who has no problem killing people, is angered at Phil's cruelty to the dog.

SCENE: An apartment in the Hollywood flats.

TIME: The present.

PHIL: That's what I'm tryin' to get at, Sal, I mean, what'd I do that for?

(*Dismayed at himself, he crosses to couch and slumps down.*)

That dog was an evil fuck, of this there's no doubt, and he had it in for me, but still. You know. I mean, he was just a nasty fuckin' little dog, but nevertheless—I mean, you know, every time I would go in there, he would growl at me, and he would bite my shoes and my trouser cuffs. I hated him. I admit it. I'm fresh out of the slam, right? The last thing I need is this goddamn dog attacking my shoes and biting my trousers, you know. I have been pent up for eight and a half years, I have kept my nose clean, then I'm out, who knows what I'm gonna do with myself, there's this goddamn dog—I mean, let's face it, let's not kid ourselves, he was a vicious little prick of a dog.

(*He lies back on couch and stretches out his hand.*)

So I fell asleep one time on Tony's couch, I'm sleepin', right? This evil fucking dog comes up to me—I got my hand like this, you know, I'm sleepin', I'm defenseless, right, this nasty little dog, he pisses on my hand. I picked him up by his collar, you know. Like he was a guy, I picked him up, I held him out, I whacked him right square between the eyes. Next thing I know, he's dead. He gets this look—it's very briefly in his eyes—this look like he has been asked a question the likes of which he has never heard of it before and he ain't got a chance in hell of gettin' it right. So he looks this way, right, and next he looks for just a second at me like he loves me, and then there's this half-second in which it appears he has just remembered a very important phone call he forgot to make, and he's gonna ask me to make it for him, or jump outa my hand and say, "Excuse me, I gotta make a phone call." So these are the looks he gives. Next thing is, this blood comin' out his eyes. I'm standin' there, I have just killed this little dog with one blow, now he's like this stuffed animal, only blood is comin' out his eyes. I thought, to myself, I don't wanna do this any more.

THREE BIRDS ALIGHTING ON A FIELD by Timberlake Wertenbaker

The vacuous pretensions of the art world are on display in this posh London gallery. A well-dressed man, the AUCTIONEER, stands on a podium next to a large canvas. The canvas is white.

SCENE: A London art auction.

TIME: The present.

AUCTIONEER: Lot 208, a painting by Theodore Quick, entitled *No Illusion*. As you can see: totally flat, authentically white. (*He looks at his audience and speaks very fast.*) I shall start this at eighty thousand pounds, eighty thousand, any advance? (*He looks.*)

Ninety thousand. One hundred thousand at the back. One hundred and twenty thousand, lady at the front. One hundred and fifty thousand. Any more?

One hundred and seventy thousand, two hundred thousand, two hundred and twenty thousand between the doors, two hundred and fifty thousand, two hundred and seventy thousand all over the place now.

Three hundred thousand at the back. Three hundred and twenty thousand, lady's bid now, at the very back, three hundred and fifty thousand, any more? Three hundred seventy thousand between the doors. Madam?

Four hundred. Four twenty, four fifty, four seventy, five hundred at the back, at the very back, yes, five hundred and twenty thousand. Five fifty, lady on my left. Five hundred and seventy thousand on the telephone. Six hundred thousand all over the place again.

Six hundred and twenty thousand, six hundred and fifty, six hundred and seventy, seven hundred, seven twenty, seven fifty at the back. Seven seventy on the telephone again. It's against you all in the room at seven seventy, seven hundred and seventy thousand.

Eight hundred thousand, eight hundred and twenty thousand, a new bidder, and now at the back, almost in the street, eight hundred and fifty thousand. Are you still in, madam? Eight hundred and seventy thousand, eight hundred and seventy thousand, nine hundred thousand at the back, nine hundred and twenty thousand, lady on my left, nine hundred and fifty thousand on the phone. Going on? No. Any more?

At the side, nine hundred and seventy, nine hundred and seventy thousand at the side, last chance at nine hundred and seventy thousand, are you going on, madam? Selling at nine hundred and seventy thousand pounds, all done? One million on the telephone.

(*A gasp.*)

One million one hundred thousand at the side, in the aisle, any more? One million two hundred thousand at the back, selling at one million two hundred thousand, all done at one million two hundred thousand pounds, one million two hundred thousand pounds: it's yours, madam.

And now Lot 209, an illuminated billboard by Laura Hellish which you can see at the back, between the doors. We can't turn on its lights but they are pink and they say: ART IS SEXY, ART IS MONEY, ART IS MONEY-SEXY, ART IS MONEY-SEXY-SOCIAL-CLIMBING-FANTASTIC, which I believe is a quote from the director of a great national museum across the water. Thirty thousand starts this. Gentleman at the back, thank you.

THE TOYER by Gardner McKay

Maude, a psychiatrist, finds herself face to face with a young man who may be the Toyer, a rapist who attacks and lobotomizes young women.

Maude allowed PETER MATSON, in his twenties, into her house. He's "lithe. Strong, not muscular. In his early twenties...Neither handsome nor ugly. Striking yet indistinct. An apparent innocent; easily written on, easily erased. A tabula rasa." He's also an actor, or so he says. As he holds Maude tightly by the neck, is it an act or the real thing?

SCENE: A one-story, one bedroom house or cottage set in Randall Canyon in the hills above Los Angeles.

TIME: A summer night.

PETER: What were *you* going to do tomorrow? Examine patients? Lunch with a doctor friend? Beat that guy Rex at tennis again? Doesn't it bother you you're not going to do any of those things? (*PETER never loses positional control over Maude.*) What about tomorrow? It's going to be different for you tomorrow. You'll be a pretty pale flower, wheeled around, fed, loved. Everyone secretly loves a failure. In a couple of days you'll start getting mail from people you don't even know, gifts—you'll watch them being opened by your family and friends. Ever thought about Saturn's moons? Nothing deader than a moon, right, but it goes on revolving, rising and setting. What about trees? Who buries a tree when it dies? No one. It stands there elegant, clean, strong. You're a good-looking woman, Maude, with a headstrong beauty. Why would I want to see you buried. Eyeless? (*Waits for a response.*) I know you don't feel chatty right now, but this is *you* we're talking about, not somebody else, don't you care? Can't you show me a couple of tears? [MAUDE: (*Whispers to herself.*) Expecting it. Always expecting it...] Strange, isn't it, your feeling of pre-destiny? All women have it, don't feel bad. [(*MAUDE sobs to herself.*)] (*Relieved.*) Good. You know, when a pack of wild dogs catches a zebra, one grips the zebra's nose in its teeth and one grips its tail, while the other wild dogs begin to eat out its stomach. It's routine. The zebra's standing on his hooves, and these dogs are eating him. You'd think he'd fight, wouldn't you? Well, he's through fighting. He's been expecting this. It's been happening to him for twenty million years and he doesn't even feel the dogs eating out his stomach. He's already gone away. (*Pause.*) Have you...gone away?

TWO TRAINS RUNNING by August Wilson

STERLING, a young black man of thirty, out of the penitentiary for one week, immediately starts courting Risa, the introverted waitress/cook of this dingy Pittsburgh restaurant. He plays the numbers so he can afford to marry her. But in order to make sure she's really the right girl, he consults the ancient fortune-teller, Aunt Ester, for guidance.

Sterling actually does win at numbers only to discover he's been cheated out of the full amount he's due. He describes his confrontation with the numbers boss, Albert—and his subsequent visit to Ester—to Risa.

SCENE: A dingy Pittsburgh restaurant where young and older blacks hang out.

TIME: 1969.

STERLING: I went up there to see old man Albert. He sitting up there with four or five bodyguards. They let me in to see him and I told him to give me back my two dollars. Said I was calling off the bet. He gave me the two dollars and asked me for his six hundred back. I told him no. Told him I was gonna keep that. That way I have something that belong to him for a change. He just looked at me funny and told me to leave the same way I had come in. Told one of his bodyguards to show me the door. I left out of there and was walking by Aunt

Ester's. I saw the light on and I figure she might be up so I stopped to see her. They led me into the hallway and then through som urtains into this room…and she was just sitting there. I talked to her a long while. Told her my whole life story. She real nice. Ain't nobody ever talk to me like that. "I cannot swim does not walk by the lake side." It took me awhile to figure out what she meant. Told me "Make better what you have and you have best." Then she wrote down something on a piece of paper, put it in a little envelope, told me to put it in my shoe and walk around on it for three days. I asked her how much I owed her. She told me to take twenty dollars and throw it in the river. Say she get it. She had this look about her real calm and sweet-like. I asked her how old she was. She say she was 349 years old. Holloway had it wrong. I figured anybody that old know what she talking about. I took twenty dollars and carried it down there. Didn't even think about it. I just took and threw it in the river. I'm gonna wait them three days and see what happen. You ought to go up there and see her. She a real nice old lady. She say yeah, you the one God sent when he told me he couldn't send no angel.

WHAT A MAN WEIGHS by Sherry Kramer

TOM HASELTINE, thirty-five, arrogant and persistent, works with Joan in a book restoring lab.

After some furious making out that led nowhere, Haseltine spends the night on the couch. But he hasn't given up.

SCENE: Joan's apartment.

TIME: The present. Morning.

HASELTINE: You know, in a way it's very comforting, to see that you have this hope. Yes, it's comforting. To see that a woman, at your age—I mean—with your—maturity—wisdom—experience—that a woman who has had and seen and done all you have can still have faith in the eternal "not yet," in the implied "later," in that better world a woman imagines she can build around a man out of the power the word "no" has when she knows both of you know it means yes.

It's a gift, to have that much faith in a word. A gift.

But I don't have it.

There's only one difference between now and later. And that's that I'm here now.

(*He kisses her.*)

Now you say you want to know something? Well here's the guy who knows.

(*He places her hand on his crotch. She doesn't exactly resist.*)

Oh, he's seen the sights all right. Been inside a couple hundred wonders of the world. Been absolutely everywhere there is for a guy like him to go. Gets into places so goddamn well fortified, the great Houdini could learn a thing or two, if he were still alive. But he wouldn't tell Houdini how he does it. They're his techniques. It's his business who he shows.

But I have the feeling that he might show you. If you ask him nicely.

(*She takes her hand off him and steps back.*)

Don't go now—don't—you got this great big burning thirst for knowledge. Don't tell me it's all burned out.

THE WRITING GAME by David Lodge

LEO RAFKIN, about fifty, American-Jewish, quite handsome in a grizzled sort of way, explains to a young writing student about good writing. Leo might be modeled on Norman Mailer.

SCENE: The Wheatcraft Centre, a seventeenth-century barn in Dorset England, converted to accommodate short residential courses in creative writing.

TIME: A recent summer.

LEO: So you see, the whole secret of writing well, is knowing when to repeat yourself and when to differ from yourself. It's something that comes unbidden, like grace... Look, I'll give you an example. In the winter of 1981, I went to Poland, just before the military takeover and the suppression of Solidarity. There were terrible shortages of food and ordinary things that we take for granted, like batteries, light bulbs, soap. After I got back home, I became obsessed with the idea of this guy who goes to Poland with a suitcase full of soap, which he uses like currency, to obtain services and favors, especially sexual ones. He uses the soap to pay prostitutes. He does kinky things with them, with the soap. I started writing the story, but I couldn't see what the point of it was, or how it could end. It was all soap and sex, soapy sex. I abandoned the story, put it away, forgot all about it. A few weeks ago I dug it out again, and as I was reading through it, I suddenly flashed on why the guy was doing this crazy stuff. Which is to say, why I had fantasized him doing it. He's Jewish, you see, like me. My family came from Poland, originally. There's a long history of persecuting Jews in that part of the world. Russians, Germans, Poles—antisemitism is about the one thing they have in common. Through the soap, by humiliating Polish *shiksas* with the soap, my character's trying to take revenge, exact reparation. His relatives would've been gassed in what they thought were shower-rooms, and their corpses boiled down to make soap. As soon as I saw that, I knew that the story would end with the guy going to visit Auschwitz and realizing what he's doing, and what it's doing to him. Soap, you see, had become a kind of pun, a serious pun. Repetition and difference compacted together. Bingo! (*grins*) Go thou and do likewise.

THE WRITING GAME by David Lodge

LEO RAFKIN, about fifty, American-Jewish, quite handsome in a grizzled sort of way, might be modeled on Norman Mailer. Leo reads his latest story for an assembly of young, impressionable writers.

SCENE: The Wheatcraft Centre, a seventeenth-century barn in Dorset England, converted to accommodate short residential courses in creative writing.

TIME: A recent summer.

LEO: This is a short story that I started several years ago, but only finished quite recently. It's called "Soap." (*Clears throat.*) "Soap." (*Reads.*)

Irving Zimmerman arrived in Warsaw with two medium-sized suitcases. One suitcase contained his clothes and lecture notes. The other was full of soap. Toilet soap. Palmolive, Lux, Camay—the basic American drugstore range, plus some imported soaps from England and France: Pears, Imperial Leather, Roger et Galet, Chanel, special handmade *trompe l'oeil* soaps in the form of fruit—apples, lemons, bananas; and soap from healthfood stores containing macrobiotic wheatgerm, almond oil, and coconut milk. The customs officer sneezed in the powerful gust of perfume that came from this suitcase when Zimmerman opened the lid.

"Why are you bringing these?" said the customs officer, pointing to the soap.

"Gifts," said Zimmerman.

"Why are you coming to Poland?"

"To lecture on American literature," said Zimmerman. "The United States Information Service sent me."

The customs official was sufficiently impressed to wave him through. Zimmerman slipped him a bar of Oil of Ulay. "For your wife," he said.

The USIS officer who had briefed him in Chicago before his trip had given Zimmerman a list of commodities he should be sure to take with him because they would be unobtainable in Poland: torch batteries, toothpaste, coffee, soap. "Coffee and toilet soap would make acceptable gifts," he added. Also barter, Zimmerman thought to himself. He went shopping for soap.

That first evening in Warsaw Zimmerman attended a cocktail party at the US Cultural Attaché's apartment, with a bar of Pink Camay bulging each pocket of his suit. He offered one to a plump, blonde lady agronomist from Lublin. She looked somewhat surprised, but slipped it dextrously into her purse, and, when they parted, rewarded him with a smacking kiss. He imagined her rushing home to take a bath with his soap, and found the thought arousing.

The Attaché gave Zimmerman dinner and delivered him to his hotel, the Europejski, a faded monument to pre-war bourgeois luxury. In the marble-floored, artdeco lobby, unaccompanied women wearing hats sat under the potted palms and crossed their legs invitingly. One of them came boldly up to Zimmerman as he collected his key from the clerk, and pretended to know him. "Hallo," she said, in English, linking her arm with his.

"How many *zlotys*?" said Zimmerman.

"*Zlotys* no good," said the girl. "Twenty dollars."

"How much soap?"

They agreed on three bars. Upstairs in his room, she took off her hat and most of her other clothes, and lay down on the bed.

"Let's take a shower together first," said Zimmerman. He fetched a lemon-shaped tablet of soap from his suitcase. "Don't worry," he said, tossing it in his hand. "This won't count as one of the three. I might even let you keep it." He had thought of a way to do this. The girl giggled and went readily enough into the bathroom.

Stripped, in the perfumed steam of the shower, she was pink and spotty and overweight. He soaped her all over, feeling her nipples spring to life under his slippery fingers. She moaned with unsimulated pleasure as he lathered her mousy quim. She squirmed on his index finger like—

(*LEO looks up as if distracted by a disturbance in the audience. He mimes watching somebody getting up and walking out. The sound of a door banging shut at the back or side of the auditorium. After a momentary pause he continues reading.*)

She squirmed on his index finger like a hooked fish. Then he bent her over the side of the tub and buggered her with the soap. She squealed as he rammed it into her. Zimmerman had never done anything like this before. He felt enormously excited. Uplifted. Then—

(*LEO breaks off again and mimes watching another person or persons walking out. The sound of the door slamming again.*)

Does anyone else want to leave?

THE WRITING GAME by David Lodge

SIMON ST. CLAIR, in his early thirties, dressed in trendy clothes, sporting an expensively styled haircut, reads from his latest work. There's a spotlight on him and his adoring students sit around him.

There's a glass of wine on the table beside him.

He holds a stack of large index cards in his hand, on each of which is written one of the numbered sections of his text. After finishing each section, he pauses and places the relevant card face down on the table.

SCENE: The Wheatcraft Centre, a seventeenth-century barn in Dorset England, converted to accommodate short residential courses in creative writing.

TIME: A recent summer.

SIMON: I'm going to read something I've been working on for some time, called *Instead of a Novel.*

(*He takes a sip of wine, then reads:*)

One. The Jacket.

The jacket is made of laminated paper printed in six colours. The front cover reproduces a painting in the style of Magritte, depicting a book held open by a pair of hands. The pages of the book are completely blank, and, mysteriously, the reader's thumbs, which should be holding the leaves down, have disappeared into the white hole of the absent text. The title, *Instead of a Novel,* runs across the top of the cover in inch-high lettering, and the name, "Simon St Clair," across the bottom, in one-and-a-half inch lettering. Underneath the name, in smaller letters of the same typeface, is the legend, "By the Author of *Wormcasts.*" Printed on the inside flap of the cover is an enthusiastic description of the contents of the book, known in the trade as the blurb.

Two. The Blurb.

"*Instead of a Novel* is, literally, indescribable. Is it an ingenious game? A shocking confession? A trap to catch the unwary reader? A dazzling display of literary virtuosity? All these things, perhaps, and more. *Instead of a Novel* fulfills the promise of Simon St Clair's brilliant and acclaimed first novel, *Wormcasts,* and sets new standards for conceptual daring and technical innovation in contemporary writing."

Three. The Photograph.

The photograph, in black and white, on the back of the jacket, is by Iain McKell, reproduced by permission of *The Face*, where it first appeared. It depicts the author in a loose ankle-length topcoat of creased grey cotton over matching baggy trousers, designed by Katherine Hamnett. He stares sulkily into the lens of the camera, leaning against a pile of damaged and obsolete juke boxes, video games, electric guitars and amplifiers, in some sordid corner of a North London junkyard.

Four. The Biographical Note.

Simon St Clair was born in 1957, and educated at Westminster School and King's College Cambridge, where he gained a First in English, and edited an alternative student newspaper called *Camshaft.* While he was still an undergraduate he began his first novel, *Wormcasts,* which was published in 1980 to widespread acclaim. It won him a Somerset Maugham Award and the Whitbread First Novel Prize. After holding various editorial posts with *Time Out,* the *New Musical Express*, and the *Listener,* he became a freelance writer, contributing reviews and articles to magazines and newspapers on both sides of the Atlantic on literature, rock music, and other aspects of contemporary culture. A collection of his essays entitled *Graffiti* was published in 1985. Simon St Clair lives in London.

Five. From the reviews of Wormcasts.

"A new and exhilarating voice in contemporary British fiction (dot, dot, dot) scintillating wit and corrosive irony."—*Observer.*

"Seldom have the pains—and pleasures—of adolescence been described with such devastating accuracy."—*The Times.*

"The thinking man's Sex Pistol."—*Guardian.*

"Possibly the most brilliant fictional debut of the decade."—*Time Out.*

(*SIMON rolls his tongue in his cheek as if to suggest that he may have inspired this last tribute himself.*)

Six. The Title Page.

INSTEAD OF A NOVEL. A novel. By Simon St Clair.

Seven. Facing the Title Page.

Other books by Simon St Clair:

Wormcasts

Graffiti

Eight. The Dedication.

To Julian, for whom it was all too much.

Nine. Acknowledgements.

To Faber and Faber Ltd for quotations from *The Waste Land* by T.S. Eliot. To Methuen & Co for quotations from *Winnie the Pooh,* by A.A. Milne. To EMI for quotations from *Wish You Were Here* by Pink Floyd. To the Cambridge Arts Cinema where I whiled away many pleasant afternoons as an undergraduate assimilating the repertoire of Godard, Fellini, Antonioni, and Hitchcock. To Amanda, Cheltenham Ladies' College and Newnham, who let me go the whole way with her after our first May Ball, or would have done if I hadn't been too drunk to perform. To Julian, who held my head as I puked into the baptismal font of the Catholic church in Hills Road on my way home, and recommended cocaine as a less bilious method of getting high. To Amanda, who gave me next Michaelmas term a second chance to have her, which I seized, and enjoyed sufficiently to repeat the exercise on many occasions, until one day she forgot to take her pill and got pregnant, and I wanted her to have an abortion, but she didn't want to, but allowed herself to be persuaded. To Julian, who borrowed from his father the money that paid for Amanda to have a quick and discreet operation in St John's Wood, after which she said she never wanted to see me again. To Julian, who nursed Amanda through her post-abortion depression so that she was able to sit Finals, and himself in consequence only got a middling Two One, instead of the First he was expected to get, and so lost his chance of a Fellowship. To Amanda, who sensibly married a lawyer from Trinity and had three children in four years. To the author of a Sunday Colour Supplement article entitled "New Contenders for the Glittering Prizes," who featured me as an up-and-coming literary genius, and to the photographer who took such a ravishing picture of me reclining in a punt in a white suit that they had to put it on the front cover. To the literary editors of London newspapers and magazines who subsequently fell over themselves to offer me work. To Verity Blackwell, genius among editors, who accepted *Wormcasts* within days of my submitting it, and wisely persuaded me to cut the scene in which the hero is fellated by a strange nun in the London Planetarium on the grounds that one could have too much of a good thing. To all my friends and acquaintances in the media, who ensured huge publicity and enthusiastic reviews for

155

Wormcasts on publication. To Julian, who wrote the only unfavourable, and only honest, review, in a little magazine that nobody reads, for which I stopped seeing him. To Amanda, who came to the launch party for *Graffiti,* gushing thanks for the invitation, and whom I fucked afterwards for old times' sake. To Julian who turned up at my flat one night, high as a kite on cocaine, and put his arms round me, and kissed me on the mouth, and told me I was the only person he had ever loved, and whom I promptly threw out, quivering with righteous indignation like an outraged Victorian maiden. To Julian, who died two years' later, a heroin addict. To all the publishers, literary editors, agents, PR men, PR women, TV producers, radio producers, record-pushers, chat-show hosts, party-givers, lunch-givers, freebie-givers, whores of every sex and profession, who have given me so many excuses to put off writing this novel.

Ten. The Epigraph.

"What draws the reader to the novel is the hope of warming his shivering life with a death he reads about."—Walter Benjamin

(*SIMON lays down the last card, looks up.*)

The rest of the book consists of two hundred and fifty completely blank pages.

Play Sources and Acknowledgements

Amsterdam,Diana. THE END OF I. In SEX AND DEATH. New York: Samuel French, Inc. 1990.

Ayckbourn, Alan. A SMALL FAMILY BUSINESS. London: Faber and Faber, 1987. Copyright © Alan Ayckbourn, 1987. Reprinted by permission of Faber and Faber.

Baitz, Jon Rob... © 1993 THE SUBSTANCE OF FIRE. New York: Samuel French, 1992.

Beane, Douglas Carter. ADVICE FROM A CATERPILLAR. New York: Samuel French, 1991.

Bell, Neal. OUT THE WINDOW. In MORE TEN-MINUTE PLAYS FROM ACTORS THEATRE OF LOUISVILLE . New York: Samuel French, 1992.

Bernstein, Douglas; Markell, Denis. SHOWBIZ RABBI. © 1989.

Blessing, Lee. FORTINBRAS. New York: Dramatists Play Service, 1992. © Copyright, 1992, by Lee Blessing. CAUTION: The reprinting of FORTINBRAS included in this volume is reprinted by permission of the author and Dramatists Play Service, Inc., 440 Park Avenue South, New York, N.Y. 10016. No stock or amateur production of the play may be given without stock obtaining in advance, the written permission of the Dramatists Play Service, Inc., and paying the requisite fee. Inquiries regarding all other rights should be addressed to Lois Berman, 240 West 44th Street, New York, N.Y. 10036.

Bottrell, David and Jones, Jessie. © 1993 DEARLY DEPARTED. New York: Dramatists Play Service, 1992.

Bozzone, Bill. ROSE COTTAGES. New York: Samuel French ,1986. © 1985, 1986 by Bill Bozzone. Reprinted by permission of the author and the Tantleff Office, 375 Greenwich St., Ste. 700, NY, NY 10013.

Brown, Carlyle, © 1992. THE LITTLE TOMMY PARKER CELEBRATED COLORED MINSTREL SHOW. New York: Dramatists Play Service, 1992. All inquiries concerning rights of any kind should be addressed in writing to the author's agent, Helen Merrill, Ltd., 435 West 23rd Street, Suite 1A, New York, NY 10011, USA. No amateur performance of this play may be given without obtaining, in advance, the written permission of Helen Merrill, Ltd.

Bullins, Ed. SALAAM, HUEY NEWTON, SALAAM. In THE BEST SHORT PLAYS 1990. New York: Applause Theatre Book Publishers, 1991. All inquiries concerning rights of any kind should be addressed in writing to the author's agent, Helen Merrill, Ltd., 435 West 23rd Street, Suite 1A, New York, NY 10011, USA. No amateur performance of this play may be given without obtaining, in advance, the written permission of Helen Merrill, Ltd.

Butterfield, Catherine. JOINED AT THE HEAD. New York: Dramatists Play Service, 1993. Copyright © Catherine Butterfield, 1992. CAUTION: The reprinting of JOINED AT THE HEAD included in this volume is reprinted by permission of the author and Dramatists Play Service, Inc., 440 Park Avenue South, New York, N.Y. 10016. No stock or amateur production of the play may be given without stock obtaining in advance, the written permission of the Dramatists Play Service, Inc., and paying the requisite fee. Inquiries regarding all other rights should be addressed to Gilbert Parker, The William Morris Agency, 1350 Avenue of the Americas, New York, New York 10019.

Cain, Bill, © 1991 STAND-UP TRAGEDY. New York: Samuel French, 1991.

Calhoun, Wil. THE BALCONY SCENE. New York: Samuel French, 1992.

Carter, Steve. SPIELE '36. Copyright © 1992.

Dorfman, Ariel, © 1991. DEATH AND THE MAIDEN. New York: Penguin Books, 1992.

Friedman, Ken, CLAPTRAP. New York: Samuel French, 1987.

Friel, Brian. AMERICAN WELCOME . Copyright © 1981 by Brian Friel. In MORE TEN -MINUTE PLAYS FROM LOUISVILLE. New York: Samuel French, 1992.

Friel, Brian. DANCING AT LUGHNASA. London: Faber and Faber Limited, 1990. Copyright © by Brian Friel. Reprinted by permission of Faber and Faber.

Gardner, Herb, © 1991. CONVERSATIONS WITH MY FATHER. C/o The author's agent, The Lantz Office, 888 Seventh Avenue, New York, New York, 10106.

Glowacki, Janusz, © 1993. ANTIGONE IN NEW YORK. C/o The author's agent, Bridget Aschenberg, International Creative Management, 40 West 57th Street, 10019.

Goluboff, Bryan, © 1993. BIG AL. C/o The author's agent, George Lane, William Morris Agency, 1350 Avenue of the Americas, New York, New York, 10019.

Goluboff, Bryan. MY SIDE OF THE STORY. Copyright © 1992. C/o The Author's Agent George Lane, William Morris, 1350 Avenue of the Americas, New York, New York 10019.

Gray, Simon, © 1993. THE HOLY TERROR. C/o The Author's Agent, William Craver, Writers and Artists Agency, 19 West 44th Street, 10036.

Greenberg, Richard, © 1991. THE AMERICAN PLAN. New York: Dramatists Play Service, 1991.

Greenberg, Richard, © 1992. THE EXTRA MAN. C/o The Author's Agent, Helen Merrill, 435 West 23rd Street, #1 A, New York, New York 10011.

Guare, John. SIX DEGREES OF SEPARATION. New York, Random House, 1990. From SIX DEGREES OF SEPARATION by John Guare. Copyright © 1990 by John Guare. Reprinted by permission of Vintage Books, a division of Random House, Inc.

Hirson, David, © 1992, 1989. LA BÊTE. New York: Dramatists Play Service, 1992.

Katims, Jason, © 1989, 1992. THE MAN WHO COULDN'T DANCE. In MORE TEN MINUTE PLAYS FROM ACTORS THEATRE OF LOUISVILLE. New York: Samuel French, 1992.

Kempinski, Tom, © 1988 [© 1989 by Glandibus Ltd.]. SEPARATION. New York: Samuel French, 1989.

Kopit, Arthur. ROAD TO NIRVANA. New York: Hill and Wang, 1992. Excerpt from ROAD TO NIRVANA by Arthur Kopit. Copyright © by Arthur Kopit 1991. Reprinted by permission of Hill and Wang, a division of Farrar, Straus & Giroux, Inc.

Korder, Howard. SEARCH AND DESTROY. New York: Grove Weidenfeld, 1992. Copyright © 1988, 1992 by Howard Kroder. Used by permission of Grove Press, Inc.

Kramer, Sherry, © 1990. WHAT A MAN WEIGHS. New York: Broadway Play Publishing, 1992.

Lee, Leslie, © 1991, 1992. BLACK EAGLES. New York: Samuel French, 1992.

Lodge, David. THE WRITING GAME. Copyright © 1991. London: Secker and Warburg, 1991.

Lucas, Craig, © 1993. CREDO and PHONE MAN. C/o The author's agent, Peter Franklin, William Morris Agency, 1350 Avenue of the Americas, New York, New York, 10019.

Mamet, David, © 1992. OLEANNA. New York: Vintage Books, 1993. Reprinted by permission of Vintage Books, a division of Random House, Inc.

Margulies, Donald, © 1992. SIGHT UNSEEN. New York: Dramatists Play Service, 1992.

Margulies, Donald, © 1989, 1990. THE LOMAN FAMILY PICNIC. New York: Dramatists Play Service , 1990.

McKay, Gardner, © 1970, 1992. TOYER. New York: Samuel French, 1992.

McNally, Terrence. LIPS TOGETHER TEETH APART. New York: New American Library, 1992. From LIPS TOGETHER TEETH APART by Terrence McNally. Copyright © 1992 by Terrence McNally. Used by permission of New American Library, a division of Penguin Books USA Inc.

McPherson, Scott. MARVIN'S ROOM. New York: New American Library, 1992. From MARVIN'S ROOM by Scott McPherson, Inroduction by Larry Kramer. Copyright © 1992 by Scott McPherson. Used by permission of New American Library, a division of Penguin Books USA Inc.

Melfi, Leonard, © 1993. BELLEVUE OF THE WEST SIDE and LAST CALL FOREVER.

Noonan, John Ford. TALKING THINGS OVER WITH CHEKHOV . New York: Samuel French, 1991.

Pielmeier, John. ON FORGETTING. In IMPASSIONED EMBRACES. New York: Dramatists Play Service. 1989. CAUTION: The reprinting of IMPASSIONED EMBRACES included in this volume is reprinted by permission of the author and Dramatists Play Service, Inc., 440 Park Avenue South, New York, N.Y. 10016. No stock or amateur production of the play may be given without stock obtaining in advance, the written permission of the Dramatists Play Service, Inc., and paying the requisite fee. Inquiries regarding all other rights should be addressed to Jeannine Edmunds, 606 N. Larchmont Blvd., #309, Los Angeles, California 90004.

Pinter, Harold. PARTY TIME. London: Faber and Faber, 1991. Copyright © 1991, Harold Pinter. Reprinted by permission of Faber and Faber.

Rabe, David, © 1993. THOSE THE RIVER KEEPS. C/o The Author's Agent, Jack Tantleff, The Tantleff Office, New York, New York 10013.

Ray, Connie; Bailey, Alan, © 1991. SMOKE ON THE MOUNTAIN. New York: Samuel French, 1991.

Reddin, Keith, © 1991. LIFE DURING WARTIME. New York: Dramatists Play Service, 1991.

Reddin, Keith, © 1991. THE INNOCENTS CRUSADE. New York: Dramatists Play Service, 1992.

Roth, Ari, © 1993. BORN GUILTY. C/o the author's agent, William Craver, Writers and Artists Agency, 19 West 44th Street, 10036.

Rudnick, Paul, © 1990, 1991. I HATE HAMLET. New York: Dramatists Play Service, 1992.

Sater, Steve, © 1991. CARBONDALE DREAMS. New York:Dramatists Play Service, 1991.

Shanley, John Patrick, © 1991. THE BIG FUNK. In 13 BY SHANLEY. New York: Applause Theatre Book Publishers, 1992.

Simon, Neil. LOST IN YONKERS. New York: Random House, 1992. From LOST IN YONKERS by Neil Simon. Copyright © 1992 by Neil Simon. Reprinted by permission of Random House, Inc.

Sondheim, Stephen; Weidman, John. ASSASSINS. New York: Theatre Communications Group, 1991. Text © 1990 and 1991 John Weidman, lyrics © 1990 and 1991 Rilting Music, Inc.

Sterner, Jerry, © 1989. OTHER PEOPLE'S MONEY. New York: Applause Theatre Books Publishers, 1990.

Stevens, David. THE SUM OF US. New York: Samuel French, 1991. Copyright © by David Stevens, 1990.

Sugarman, Robert © 1993. THE GLORIOUS FOURTH. C/o

Szentgyorgyi, Tom, © 1990. DINOSAUR DREAMS, C/o Tom Szentygiorgyi, Denver Center Theatre Company 1050 13th St. Denver, CO 80204.

Tesich, Steve. SQUARE ONE. New York: Applause Theatre Book Publishers, © 1990.

Tesich, Steve. ON THE OPEN ROAD. New York: Applause Theatre Book Publishers, © 1992.

Warner, Craig. BY WHERE THE OLD SHED USED TO BE. In BEST RADIO PLAYS OF 1989. London: Methuen, 1990. Copyright © 1989 by Craig Warner. Reprinted by permission of Methuen London.

Wertenbaker, Timberlake. THREE BIRDS ALIGHTING ON A FIELD, © 1991. London: Faber and Faber Limited, 1992.

Wesley, Richard, © 1989. THE TALENTED TENTH. C/o The Author's Agent, Mary Meagher, The Gersh Agency, 103 West 42nd Street, New York, New York 10036.

Whitacre, Bruce E. A GENTILE OF THE TOP PERCENTILE. C/o Bruce E. Whitacre. C/o The Manhattan Theatre Club, 453 West 16th Street, New York, New York 10011.

Wilson, August. TWO TRAINS RUNNING. New York: Dutton, 1993. From TWO TRAINS RUNNING by August Wilson. Copyright © 1992 by August Wilson. Used by permission of the publisher, Dutton, an imprint of New American Library, a division of Penguin Books USA Inc.

Wilson, Lanford. A POSTER OF THE COSMOS. New York: Dramatists Play Service, 1990. © Copyright, 1990 by Lanford Wilson. A POSTER OF THE COSMOS © Copyright, 1988, by Lan ford Wilson as an unpublished dramatic composition. CAUTION: Professionals and amateurs are hereby warned that A POSTER OF THE COSMOS are subject to a royalty. They are fully protected under the copyright laws of the United States of America, and of all countries covered by the International Copyright Union (including the Dominion of Canada and the rest of the British Commonwealth), and of all countries covered by the Pan-American Copyright Convention and the Universal Copyright Convention, and of all countries with which the United States has reciprocal copyright relations. All rights, including professional, amateur, motion picture, recitation, lecturing, public reading, radio broadcasting, television, video or sound taping, all other forms of mechanical or electronic reproduction, such as information storage and retrieval systems and photocopying and the rights of translation into foreign languages, are strictly resesrved. Particular emphasis is laid upon the question of readings, permission for which must be secured from the author's agent in writing—The stage perfomance rights A POSTER OF THE COSMOS (other than first class right) are controlled exclusively by the DRAMATISTS PLAY SERVICE, INC., 440 Park Avenue South, New York, New York 10016. No professional or non-professional performance of the play (excluding first class professional performance) may be given without obtaining in advance the written permission of the DRAMATISTS PLAY SERVICE, INC., and paying athe requisite fee—Inquiries concerning all other rights should be addressed to Bridgetg Aschenberg, International Creative Management, Inc., 40 West 57th Street, New York, New York 10019. (The length of this notice does not imply that similar protections do not apply to other plays in this book.)

Michael Caine • John Cleese
Eric Bentley • John Houseman
Michael Chekhov • John Patrick Shanley
Cicely Berry • John Russell Brown
Jerry Sterner • Steve Tesich
Harold Clurman • Sonia Moore
Bruce Joel Rubin • Jonathan Miller
Josef Svoboda • Terry Jones
Stephen Sondheim • Larry Gelbart

These Applause authors have their work available
in discerning bookshops across the globe.

If you're having trouble tracking down an Applause title in your area, we'll ship it to you direct!

U.S. Customers: Include the price of the
book, $2.95 for the first book and $1.90 thereafter to cover shipping
(NY and TN residents:
include sales tax).
Check/Mastercard/Visa/Amex

Send your orders to: **Applause Direct**
211 West 71st St
New York, NY 10023
212-595-4735
Fax: 212-721-2856

U.K. Customers: Include £1.25 p&p for first title and 25p for each additional title.
Cheque/Master/Visa

Send your order to: **Applause Direct**
406 Vale Road
Tonbridge KENT
TN9 1XR
0732-357755
Fax: 0732-770219

Write or call for our free catalog of cinema and theatre titles.

APPLAUSE
BOOKS